Praise for *Horses with a Mission*

"The stories in *Horses with a Mission* demonstrate the soul presence in horses as they use their innate creativity, sensitivity, and intelligence to make choices that serve themselves and others. Karen Sussman's account of rescuing and documenting a wild horse herd reminds all of us that native and indigenous horses have been here for 52 million years. With hearts and minds open, we can learn from the wild and domesticated horses in this wonderful book."

— Joe Camp, author of *The Soul of a Horse*
and creator of the films starring canine superstar Benji

"*Horses with a Mission* allows us to travel into the world of the horse from so many unique perspectives and introduces horses that have touched and changed the lives of many people. To have our own writer, Cooky McClung, featured in this wonderful work makes it all the more fun. It's a fabulous read."

— Mason Phelps, Jr., president, PhelpsSports.com

"As an equine professional teaching in seven countries for over forty years, I have read and witnessed many inspirational, magical, and wonderful interactions between horses and humans. *Horses with a Mission* is an exceptional collection of such stories. The contributors show fine writing abilities and talent and share the deep appreciation and love they have for their equine counterparts. Bravo. Enjoy!"

— Franklin Levinson, www.WayoftheHorse.org

"Many pets are here on this earth to help humans in the journey of life. Horses, with their primal nature as prey animals, daily make choices to override their fears, get past traumas, and put themselves in danger to be one with the humans who love them. The stories in this book are great examples of the power of unconditional love, which I am reminded of every day in my work helping clients."

— Lydia Hiby, animal communicator

"This brilliant compilation of lovely and touching stories reflects upon the remarkable connection between humans and equines. You don't need to be an avid equestrian like me to truly enjoy this book, as the stories resonate with a spirit of hope and harmony that is shared by all creatures great and small."

— Alison Eastwood, actress, director, and producer

"Through their courage, sensitivity, kindness, and so many other characteristics, the horses in this book become our inspiration and guides. I was especially taken with the way each story gives us something to reflect on in our own lives. And each chapter ends with an invitation to follow up on what we've just felt and experienced, a way to experience quiet time with these magical beings."

— Michael Mountain, former president of
Best Friends Animal Society

Praise for *Angel Horses: Divine Messengers of Hope*

"If you love horses and appreciate the countless gifts they bring to our lives, you will want to keep this exceptional collection of heartwarming stories close to your bedside for inspirational reading. *Angel Horses* is a rare gift to the world of equines."

— Linda Tellington-Jones,
founder of the Tellington TTouch Method

"The stories in *Angel Horses* are told with passion and insight into the horse-human bond."

— Anna Banks, PhD, equine massage practitioner
and editor of www.womentalkhorses.com

horses

with a Mission

Also by Allen and Linda Anderson

Angel Animals: Divine Messengers of Miracles

Angel Animals Book of Inspiration:
Divine Messengers of Wisdom and Compassion

Angel Cats: Divine Messengers of Comfort

Angel Dogs: Divine Messengers of Love

Angel Horses: Divine Messengers of Hope

Rainbows and Bridges: An Animal Companion Memorial Kit

Rescued: Saving Animals from Disaster

Saying Goodbye to Your Angel Animals:
Finding Comfort After Losing Your Pet

horses
with a Mission

Extraordinary True
Stories of Equine Service

ALLEN *and* LINDA ANDERSON

New World Library
Novato, California

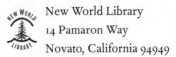 New World Library
14 Pamaron Way
Novato, California 94949

Text design by Tona Pearce Myers

Library of Congress Cataloging-in-Publication Data
Horses with a mission : extraordinary true stories of equine service / [edited by] Allen & Linda Anderson.
    p.   cm.
Includes bibliographical references.
ISBN 978-1-57731-648-0 (pbk. : alk. paper)
    1. Horses—Behavior—Anecdotes. 2. Altruistic behavior in animals—Anecdotes. I. Anderson, Allen. II. Anderson, Linda C.
SF281.H67 2009
636.1—dc22   2009022208

First printing, September 2009
ISBN 978-1-57731-648-0
Printed in Canada on 100% postconsumer-waste recycled paper

New World Library is a proud member of the Green Press Initiative.

10 9 8 7 6 5 4 3 2 1

Contents

Chapter Four: Healing

Chapter Five: Bringing Joy and Hope

INTRODUCTION

The horses show him nobler powers;
O patient eyes, courageous hearts!

— JULIAN GRENFELL

Fascinating, mystifying, highly intelligent — horses have evoked awe in humans for thousands of years. The annals of history and literature speak of equines who made adventure, power, and the fulfillment of dreams possible for humans and entire cultures. *Horses with a Mission: Extraordinary True Stories of Equine Service* focuses on an aspect of horses that remains unexplored in today's utilitarian world: horses as vibrant spiritual beings, infused with purpose and intention. The book's stories about the divine essence of horses allow glimpses into their secret worlds.

Horses excel at making history. They settled foreign lands, fought in wars, delivered people and goods to their destinations, herded cattle, and performed countless other useful and necessary endeavors. Riding a horse gives a person an imperial perspective that can only be gained from high atop a horse's back. The American Museum of Natural History's webpage devoted to its horse exhibit states, "Some cultures have considered horses worthy of gods. In many faiths, they play a role in sacred rituals. Swift, strong and sometimes unruly, a spirited horse can be awe-inspiring. A running horse may be seen as an expression of freedom, a rearing horse as a symbol of power."[1]

People regularly speak of horses' sensitivity, independence, flight-or-fight instincts, herd mentality, agility, strength, speed, and breathtaking beauty. This book invites readers to take notice of the horse's more esoteric aspects, such as free will, creativity, gratitude, humor, patience, courage, and compassion. Looking beyond the familiar landscape of equine personality, physicality, and emotions, these stories turn our faces to the promising sunrise of viewing Horse as soul.

Horse History

The first members of the horse family roamed North American forests 55 million years ago and went extinct in that part of the world about 10,000 years ago. Horses were reintroduced to the Americas by the Spanish Conquistadors. Native Americans quickly fell in love with this highly adaptable and resourceful species. Well suited to doing the work humans demanded of them, with their muscular bodies powered only by grass or hay and their instinctual abilities to read subtle cues, horses became vehicles for both the conquerors and the conquered to achieve their goals.

With more than 58 million horses worldwide, composed of hundreds of breeds and types, the bond between humans and horses endures long after most of the practical benefits of the relationship have faded. On most of the globe, horses no longer plow fields, deliver mail, or ride into battle, except in movie spectaculars. Yet a primal human-horse connection continues. The International Museum of the Horse website says:

> According to the American Horse Council, in 2001 there were approximately 6.1 million horses and 7.1 million people involved in the horse industry in the U.S. The same survey indicated that the horse industry directly produces goods and services of $25.3 billion and has a total impact

of over $112 billion on the U.S. gross domestic product. The industry's contribution to the U.S. GDP is greater than the motion picture, railroad, and furniture and fixtures manufacturing industries. It is only slightly smaller than the apparel and other textile products manufacturing industry. The industry pays a total of $1.9 billion in taxes to federal, state and local governments.[2]

Much more than being good for the economy, though, horses forge unique paths of extraordinary service. They become catalysts for people to give of themselves to others. The horses you are about to meet are vehicles for life-changing journeys, service, inspiration, teaching, healing, joyfulness, and hope.

Unusual Gifts of Service

While researching this book, we came across accounts of horses who provide gifts of love and service in fields where you just wouldn't expect to find a horse as a major player. Following are a few examples of unusual and thought-provoking horse endeavors.

Renée's Cholla

In our previous book, *Angel Horses: Divine Messengers of Hope* (New World Library, 2005), we included the story, "The Artist Is a Horse," about a Reno, Nevada, mustang named Cholla. Since then, Cholla's paintings have been exhibited in many art galleries. People can watch Cholla painting at www.artistisahorse.com. His painting *The Big Red Buck* made national news in a *USA Today* article by Sandra Chereb when it was selected for exhibit in the 3rd International Art Prize Arte Laguna in Mogliano Veneto, Italy, out of 3,000 pieces of artwork entered in the 2008 competition.[3]

Renée Chambers offered Cholla a brush, some paints, and a canvas on a hunch that he would enjoy painting in his peaceful pasture. She says about his mission:

> More and more, we humans acknowledge the pure intelligence that animals possess. Animals are attuned to the universe with a sixth sense of awareness due to their focus on survival always taking center stage. Cholla, my horse, the artist, a survivor with a mustang heritage, is no exception. However, his intelligence tells him he is safe and secure now, which allows him to extend his expression. Cholla is a serious artist. He holds a true artist's brush with his teeth and paints at his easel. He wasn't trained to paint. He is an established artist, and his recognition by the art world praises horses everywhere.[4]

In 2005, Jeanie and Tim Clifford started the nonprofit charity Back in the Saddle Bit by Bit (B.I.T.S.) in Broomfield, Colorado. The Cliffords are experienced in helping people with physical and mental challenges to excel in horseback riding and improve their motor skills and cognitive abilities through equine therapy techniques. They decided to focus on assisting military personnel who had suffered injuries while serving their country; they formed B.I.T.S. to accomplish this goal. The organization's specially trained horses, instructional staff, volunteers, and team of doctors aid veterans in their recovery.[5]

Meghan E. Moravcik reports in an article for the *Arizona Republic* that Stable Influence Charity Programs brought two of its horses to the Glendale American Elementary School to teach math to 90 seventh graders. In small groups the students approached the horses and were taught how to measure the animals' height and weight. The school principal rode one of the horses to motivate the students even more in this creative math lesson.[6]

Did you know that miniature horses are being trained to guide the blind and assist people who have physical disabilities? Evidently, miniature horses can provide an ideal solution for blind horse lovers who have allergies to or fears about dogs. These calm horses with excellent memory and vision live longer than dogs and provide strong support to someone who is trying to rise from a chair. Not affiliated with any dog guide training organizations, according to its website at www.guidehorse.com, the Guide Horse Foundation's mission is "to provide a safe, cost-effective and reliable mobility alternative for visually impaired people. The Guide Horse Foundation is committed to delivering Guide Horses at no cost to the blind, relying on unpaid volunteers and charitable donations to pay all travel and housing expenses for the blind handler's on-site training."[7]

Charlie McGuire, RN, MA, HNP, founded the American Holistic Nurses Association (AHNA). Before Charlie died, she and her partner Robbie Nelson, OTR, bought the Buffalo Woman Ranch in Dove Creek, Colorado. There, nurses pair with equine partners for exercises inspired by Linda Kohanov's Equine Facilitated Integrated Healing methods to help them become more authentic and aware in their personal lives and professions.[8]

In an article for the *Hartford Courant*, Bill Leukhart wrote about dwarf miniature Thumbelina, the world's smallest horse, measuring at 17.5 inches, 59 pounds. Thumbelina makes more than two hundred appearances annually at pediatric cancer units, burn centers, museums, and other public and private events. The horse is driven in the Thumbymobile and taken around the country by co-owner Mike Goessling, former St. Louis, Missouri, rock club owner. Goessling's helper Will Porter claims Thumbelina is much easier to deal with than rock musicians.[9]

Horses contribute to their human communities by serving on modern-day posse teams, performing search-and-rescue operations, controlling crowds, and providing positive public relations for law enforcement departments and mounted police patrols.

Horses work in hundreds of therapeutic riding programs, many of which are accredited by the North American Riding for the Handicapped Association (NARHA). They provide hippotherapy, a technique in which trained and licensed physical or occupational therapists guide a child or adult with physical disabilities to let a horse's natural movement increase his or her mobility and balance. Side benefits often include greater self-esteem and mental function. Equine-assisted psychotherapy and equine-facilitated learning are two types of programs in which intuitive horses, adept at reading human behavior and emotions, act as mirrors to individuals who want to learn more about their true feelings.

So if you ever thought that horses only display their abilities on race tracks, in riding stables, in beer commercials, in movies, or as participants in sporting events, you're missing out on their ever-expanding services as sentient partners and willing coworkers.

Horses Finding Their True Callings

In this book we introduce you to some of the most amazing horses on the planet. You'll meet horses who have saved people's and animals' lives, welcomed novices into the horse world, brought joy and comfort to the brokenhearted, made it possible for people to fulfill lifelong ambitions, and became symbols and examples of giving without expecting a return. These horses are change agents. They help their human companions view life from an expanded and higher perspective. At times, the horses have affected one or two people; in other instances, they have touched hearts around the world. Always, they gave love and devotion to someone who needed it.

The following are previews from some of the twenty-one dramatic true stories that amazed and delighted us:

Sankofa, a wise-beyond-his-years stallion, made it possible for social studies teacher Miles J. Dean to complete a cross-country journey in tribute to African American ancestors. Millions of adults and schoolchildren followed their odyssey as Miles and Sankofa made history come alive.

Molly, a pony whom Kaye T. Harris rescued after Hurricane Katrina, showed such spunkiness and courage in spite of her loss of a leg, surgery, and prosthetic device that she inspired the people of New Orleans and admirers around the world. Now Molly and Kaye visit children's hospitals, nursing homes, and other places that invite them to spread their messages of hope.

Butch, a retired gelding working with the Snow Mountain Ranch Therapeutic Riding program in Colorado, showed such an unswerving belief in a profoundly mentally retarded child that he restored Jodi Buchan's hopes for her child's future.

Pegasus, a rage-bound gelding, found his calling, to the delight and relief of his owner, Vanessa Wright, after unexpectedly taking a foal under his wings and from that point on caring for all the young horses who came into his pasture.

Peanut, an elderly and forgetful horse who had been the favorite playmate of Cooky McClung's children, lost his youth and usefulness until he connected with a kindred human counterpart and brought joy and conversation to both their final days.

Rocky, an injured young Percheron, became one of the first success stories to gain community support for the Amish Horse Retirement Program started by Annette Fisher, executive director of Happy Trails Farm Animal Sanctuary.

Diana and her rare Gila herd of wild horses were rescued by Karen Sussman, president of International Society for the Protection of Mustangs and Burros. This proud and resourceful lead mare protected her herd and taught the great lesson of forgiveness.

Terminology and Horse People

Although it's been our policy in other books we have written about animals not to refer to people as owners, writing a horse book requires using ownership terminology. Plainly and simply, in today's world, horses are bought and sold. Still we hold the opinion that it is not possible to own any animal as if it were a commodity. The spirit of a horse can't be possessed just because money has been exchanged.

For those readers who aren't owned by a horse but find them fascinating, we have asked contributing authors to define horse terminology in their stories. In general, when describing the size of a horse, the term *hands* is used. A hand is approximately the size of a hand, or 4 inches. Horses are measured by starting from the ground and placing the palm of your hand vertically against the horse while pointing your fingers at the tail and moving your hand up to the horse's shoulders, or withers.

Volumes are written about training horses. It seems to us that the most successful methods, such as natural horsemanship, use the horse's instinctive need to be part of a herd. By learning the language and culture of horse society and its family structures, humans can win horses' loyalty, cooperation, and affection. These stories prove the point that horses form willing and respectful partnerships with people when allowed and encouraged to do so.

In our first horse book, *Angel Horses: Divine Messengers of Hope,* we wrote that we had observed two types of horse people: the ones who get it and the ones who don't. By *it*, we were referring to the awareness that horses are intelligent, emotional, sentient, and creative individuals. The horse people who don't get it apply harsh and intimidating training methods and dispose of their horses as soon as they are no longer useful or capable of making returns on investments. We received letters from readers who expressed agreement with our initial observations. Of course, the contributing authors in this book are those who definitely get it. We invite you to go to the Contributors section, read the authors' short biographies, write to them about their stories, and support their missions.

Join us now on this adventure into a world in which we encourage you to experience horses in an entirely new way. It is our honor to present horses fulfilling extraordinary missions while revealing their true essence as beacons of light, messengers of love and service.

CHAPTER ONE

Offering Service

At my door the pale horse stands
To carry me to unknown lands.

— JOHN MILTON HAY

UNDER THE WINGS OF PEGASUS

VANESSA WRIGHT, *Nashua, New Hampshire*

The first rays of dawn were beginning to light the face of the sleeping world as I pulled into the barn's silent parking lot. I turned off my truck ignition and smiled wryly, waiting for the unique reveille that the resident barn staff had come to depend on for their alarm clock: the *rattle-rattle-thump* of my old Chevy's battered engine, followed by an imperious "Feed me!" whinny from my horse, Pegasus.

As I jumped down from the running board, the engine settled with a final thump and a sudden, shrill creak that startled a flock of pigeons from their roost on the barn's roof. The birds scolded me with their hoots, but strangely I heard no retort of joyful welcome from Pegasus.

Perplexed, I scanned the high hill that was Pegasus's pasture. When Pegasus — at 17 hands and 1,200 pounds, and the color of newly polished silver — galloped out of his shed, his mane, tail, and feathers streaming, racing to be the first to breakfast, he usually shone against the shadowed woods like a shooting star. This morning, though, the pasture was empty and silent. My memory flickered back to a February morning several years ago, the only other time Pegasus had failed to greet me.

A Problem with No Easy Solution

Leading up to that February morning, the trouble had begun when I brought Pegasus to our new barn. In hand and under saddle, Pegasus was a perfect gentleman. Even the barn owner's four-year-old daughter could lead him, groom him, and sneak the occasional swing from his tail. But when his work was done, and we turned him out, he became our and the other horses' nightmare. The simple fact was that Pegasus refused to tolerate the presence of other horses.

Certainly at this large barn they'd had turnout troubles before. Usually, though, once new horses had spent a few days sharing a fence line with their soon-to-be herdmates and had a chance to bond separately with an established member of the herd, they then folded into the larger group without much fanfare. But Pegasus was different. Even sharing a fence line seemed to goad him into a fury. From his very first day he would charge the electric fences, leap the stone walls, and crash through the four-board two-by-fours to get into the other pastures. Once inside, he would chase or attack any horse — mare, gelding, or stallion — in his path.

We tried every kind of care and diet modification and several types of positive behavior training to help Pegasus accept other horses. In the end, though, there was nothing we could do but pasture him alone. The barn owner and I surveyed a little more than an acre on the high hill and surrounded it with a five-foot, four-rail fence. Each rail was a six-inch-thick muscled arm of lodge-pole pine, sleeved with a 4,000-volt hotwire. Trees bordered the pasture on three sides; on the fourth was an old, unused dry lot with a shed that we renovated to create a cozy all-weather shelter.

The pasture and pine fence had held Pegasus for nearly all of his first year until that one morning in February. When I arrived at the barn my engine had settled with a frosty clank, but Pegasus had not come down to greet me. Threading my way through the snowdrifts, I had found him at last, standing inside the shed, his right hind leg a mass of shredded flesh, his fetlock, the grapefruit-sized ankle joint, gashed to the bone. Too shocked to whinny, too injured to move, he had stood there, glazed-eyed and trembling, a slow pool of scarlet spreading in the snow under his hooves.

A few hours later, while the veterinarian finished stitching Pegasus's wounds, the barn owner and I pieced together what had happened. One of the geldings had been turned out in the dry lot for a few minutes while the road to the big pasture was being plowed, and Pegasus had kicked straight through the top rail of the wooden fence to get to him. The rail lay in the snow in two neat pieces, as easily snapped as if it were a toothpick. The barn owner and I thought that a stronger fence might be the solution. We replaced the wooden fence with a metal one, and ran it through the shed that the pasture and dry lot shared. Through the spring and summer, the new fence had held Pegasus. But that autumn, after a lesson pony had gotten loose and galloped a few triumphant laps around the farm, the barn owner and I found some of the metal fence rails not broken but bizarrely twisted and bent. Stepping back a few paces, we gasped. The damage formed a perfect outline of a horse charging as swiftly, madly, and unheedingly as a comet into but not through the solid steel rails.

The barn owner whistled softly. "Someday, something's going to singe that horse's wings," she muttered, "and no fence in this world will be stronger than his fury."

What Would I Find This Time?

All these thoughts of my horse's previous run-ins with fences flashed through my mind this day as I sprinted down the gravel path toward Pegasus's pasture. My heart leapt in my chest, and I began to run. My hands shook as I unlatched the gate. I had only one question: Had my horse finally torn through steel?

When I barreled up the high pasture hill, my worst fears seemed to be confirmed. I could see Pegasus silhouetted in his shed, standing as perfectly, terribly still as he had that past February when he'd been wounded by breaking the wooden fence. Only this time, I knew, a run in with the metal fence would have left him with more severe injuries than he had suffered previously. If he had flung himself hard enough into the fence, he would have cracked ribs or bruised organs. And if he had kicked it, his leg, not the rail, would be snapped in two.

Without breaking stride, I pulled my cell phone from my pocket and pressed the speed dial for the vet. But as I approached the open side of the shed, Pegasus suddenly swung his head toward me. He flipped his muzzle at me twice and then fluttered his nostrils in a silent whinny.

I stopped and shut off my phone. I glanced over Pegasus's body, searching for an injury and wondering what had transfixed him so completely since his head, neck, back, and belly were whole and unharmed. Behind him, the metal rails of the fence that divided the shed were straight and shining, completely untouched.

Vanessa's Pegasus

And then I saw it. Saw the impossible. Poking out from under the lowest rail on the other side of the metal fence that divided the shed, with his head and front legs stretched under the fence and blissfully tangled around Pegasus's hind hooves, there rested a tiny, peach-fuzzed muzzle and two china-teacup hooves.

I tiptoed, almost lightheaded with disbelief, to Pegasus's side. He curled his neck around me as I crouched down next to him and the two of us stared in wonder. The little face and delicate legs belonged to a scrawny brown foal who was no more than a week or two old. Nestled sweetly, the foal was sound asleep, his baby breaths making Pegasus's silver feathers dance.

I rose as quietly as I could. Looking for the foal's mother, I peered into the dry lot, which adjoined but was separate from Pegasus's pasture. Having left her foal behind, she was staggering toward the dry lot's gate at the foot of the hill on her side of the fence. With her lips to the ground, she scrabbled for the tiniest bits of leftover hay. Her ribs stood out from her body like cruel, flesh-less fingers, prodding her relentlessly away from her beloved baby with her even more desperate need for food.

I gripped Pegasus's mane, though I doubted I could stop him if he decided to charge. But Pegasus only watched the mare with calm eyes and made no move.

The door to the apartment above the barn clattered open then, and one of the barn staff emerged to give the horses their morning feed. Seeing her, Pegasus stretched out his neck, extended his nose to its utmost, and pricked his ears as far forward as they could go. Still, this horse, whose stomach good horsemen set their clocks by, didn't move or make a sound, allowing the exhausted foal to sleep on, undisturbed.

A few minutes later, when the girl drove the hay cart toward the pasture gates, which were about thirty feet apart along the same fence line, the mare raised her eyes from the dust and chaff and whinnied. At the mare's call, the foal awakened and, blinking blearily, scrambled to his feet.

For the first time in the five years that I had known him, Pegasus turned his attention away from an approaching hay cart. Then, perhaps for the first time in his life, he gazed with kindness at a horse, this gaunt and gawky slip of a foal on the other side of the metal fence.

Gently, Pegasus arched his neck over the metal rails and touched the foal's nose with his. He watched as the foal tottered out of his side of the shed and down the hill and stuck his head resolutely under his mama. Satisfied, Pegasus nudged me with his head, and the two of us trotted down to his pasture gate, where he neighed like thunder for his breakfast, awaiting the hay cart's arrival.

I asked the girl about the mare and foal. "It was a rescue case," she said, throwing several fat flakes of hay over the fence. "They came in last night, and this was the only space we had."

I had planned to bring Pegasus in for a morning ride but decided instead to wait and see what would happen. One of the hay flakes had landed slightly under the fence that divided the two pastures. The foal watched as Pegasus dug into the hay with gusto. Tentatively first, then boldly, the foal thrust his muzzle under the bottom rail of the fence, into Pegasus's hay pile, lipping and nipping the leafy stems. Pegasus, who usually would have defended his hay to the death, only snorted once and kept chewing stolidly and contentedly.

When the hay was gone, Pegasus walked, trotted, and cantered with the foal along their shared fence line. And when the morning had passed and a sultry, late summer afternoon had settled in its place, the foal curled up in Pegasus's shadow and napped. Though the sun beat down on him, and the plump, sweet valley grass and cool shade of the shed beckoned, Pegasus once again stood still, watching over the little horse, providing shelter for the foal's big horse dreams.

Pegasus Finds His Calling

During the next eight months, a new, vast expanse of Pegasus's spirit unfurled. He became nanny and tutor, coach and leader of their herd of two. Racing him along their fence line, the spindly brown foal of indeterminate breed quickly grew into a strapping bay quarter horse colt. By turns playfully pummeling Pegasus with his pearl-like hooves and submitting happily to long sessions of mutual grooming, the once-forlorn baby matured into a confident young horse. He grew full of the natural joy and boldness — touched by a sparkling streak of mischief — that belong by right to youth.

Soon it came time to wean the colt. The clear choice for his first buddy was his great silver guardian, Pegasus. The barn owner, the staff, the colt's owner, and I were present to supervise. We took a deep breath and turned the two out together in Pegasus's pasture. The colt pranced immediately to Pegasus's side, ran his chin from Pegasus's withers to his flanks, and nipped him fearlessly and sharply on the rump. Pegasus's eyes popped open and he kicked half-heartedly. Then the two of them once again touched noses and ambled off, side by side, to tuck into a patch of juicy clover.

From that day on, Pegasus shared his pasture with the colt, playing with him, teaching him manners, and chaperoning his playdates with the cats, the dogs, and the flock of wild turkeys who began dropping by to visit. On sunny afternoons, the colt still curled up in Pegasus's shadow to nap. But when it rained, the colt would either cuddle against Pegasus's enormous, warm side or flop down under my horse's belly and snooze.

Pegasus always stayed awake while the colt slept and seemed to keep a constant eye on him. But I could tell, as with anyone who cares for the young, that loving attention sometimes took its toll. One day, I found the colt frolicking alone among the buttercups and daisies by the woods' edge. Pegasus had moseyed down to the water trough for a drink and had dozed off with his head balanced precariously on the trough's rim.

These were happy times, but eventually the colt's owner found him a forever home. And while the colt began a joyful new chapter of his life, shortly after he moved away, Pegasus started to decline. He stopped eating. He drank next to nothing. Most heartbreaking of all, he spent hours wandering anxiously around his pasture, whinnying piteously into the empty sky.

Finally, one day a few weeks later, his whinny was answered. A friend's palomino filly lost her mother, so the little golden girl took up residence on the hill. Pegasus befriended and raised her. After she grew up, he went on to parent many others, colts and fillies of every background and breed. As the years passed, Pegasus grew into a true healer: he helped his foals become whole and sound and also restored himself. This once-friendless gelding created a family and a legacy that is truly his own. My previously rage-bound horse had let love teach him how to fly.

Now when I arrive at the barn and Pegasus is nowhere in sight, I don't worry. I know he is guarding the dreams of another young horse, keeping bright the vision of the wonderful future he or she has ahead. He is their great, silver angel, and they can grow and rest, safe and content, under the span of his mighty wings.

MEDITATION

The transition from anger to offering hope and joy replaced Pegasus's negativity with love and friendship. How have you had a change of heart or attitude by giving of yourself to others?

MOLLY, THE THREE-LEGGED PONY
WHO GAVE HOPE TO NEW ORLEANS
❧

KAYE T. HARRIS, *New Orleans, Louisiana*

I did my first volunteer work for the Royal SPCA in Singapore when I was eleven years old, and I have always been one to rescue animals. After Hurricane Katrina hit, my husband Glenn and I ran a food line in our parish just outside New Orleans with volunteer ministers. One day, we traveled into New Orleans to drop off supplies for hurricane victims at various locations. Our pony ride business has trucks used to transport the ponies, and our volunteers loaded these up with food, water, and ice.

After delivering the supplies, we stopped at our feed store to see if we could find feed for our animals. Ginger, the owner, was helping rescued animals who were sheltered at the store. She said that there was a pony who had been left behind when Hurricane Katrina hit and was being cared for by the Arizona Humane Society while that group worked in New Orleans. No one had a trailer to transport the pony, and the volunteers were leaving and could no longer care for her. Ginger asked if I could take the pony. She thought I'd be the perfect person, since I was a pony expert with twenty ponies at the time. I agreed to rescue the pony.

My husband and I went to pick up the pony from her barn on September 6, 2005, which was my birthday. We were surprised to find that a tree had fallen halfway through her stall. I don't know how she had not been killed. It amazed me that already she had survived both a hurricane and her stall being smashed by a tree. I was soon to find out how much more of a survivor this pony would be.

Upon first meeting the pony, I observed that she was predominately black but shot through with white roan hairs. Turns out, she is a Pony of the Americas, with Appaloosa mottling around her eyes and nose. Her mane and tail are mostly black, with silver and white hairs throughout. She is forty-four inches tall at the withers. At the time we estimated her age at fifteen.

Our ponies are all trained to jump into the back of our trucks, and there are racks for transporting them. On the day we brought the pony home, we backed up to one of our levees so this plucky survivor would have a very small distance over which to jump into the truck bed. This girl did not hesitate and leapt right inside. It was like she was saying, "I'm leaving!" We left a note for her owners with our phone number.

This smart pony rode perfectly all the way home. She got down from the truck with no problem. For the next couple of months she pastured with my herd of older horses. When her owners returned, they turned ownership of her over to us. We then found out our survivor's name: Molly.

Molly's Disaster

After we brought Molly home, my husband and I rescued other displaced Hurricane Katrina animals until after Thanksgiving. I personally rescued a pit bull terrier. Instead of leaving him at the MuttShack Animal Rescue Triage Center in New Orleans, where I was volunteering, I brought him home. We called him Red Sam. After all he had endured, it was not surprising that the dog had severe anxiety attacks. Whenever we left him alone in our house, he would chew or tear up something, but it was always an inanimate object, like the floor or items in my son's bedroom.

I thought that being with other people or animals might relieve Red Sam's anxiety. He had never shown any signs of aggression toward other animals in my presence. However, because of all the fear, pain, and near-death he had experienced, the dog had what I now know as post-Katrina syndrome. It resulted in his acting out violently in a way that I had never imagined possible and would lead to a mistake that I regret to this day

On December 3, 2005, I had to make a quick trip to the post office. I left Red Sam loose in the front yard with the rest of the dogs, which is something I should not have done. Upon my return I saw Red Sam lunging and barking at Molly in her paddock. She was lying down. At first I didn't think much of it, because our dogs will bark at the horses, so I told him to leave Molly alone. Then I watched, horrified, as he grabbed on to Molly's jaw.

Molly with Kaye (left) and Makaila Valentine at Camp Rap-A-Hope

I ran for the four-foot fence and hurdled over it. I called the dog, and he got right off Molly. He went back under the fence into the other yard. But Molly couldn't get up. Red Sam had not only gnawed through her right front leg but also had inflicted wounds on all four legs. He'd slit a deep gash in her belly and torn her jaw. She was going into shock. I bent down to hold her bleeding jaws together.

I was in a pure, unadulterated state of panic. Molly breathed hard, gasping for air. Now that I was closer I could see the reason she had been lying down. During the dog's attack on her, he'd chewed her legs so badly that she couldn't get up.

Because of the hurricane, our cell phone coverage remained

spotty. I prayed that I could get a signal long enough to call my veterinarian's emergency number, leave a message, and wait for her to phone back. (The vet is Allison D. Barca, DVM, who practices in the greater New Orleans area. We are also good friends, and Allison is now Molly's godmother. If something happened to me, Allison would take care of Molly.) Within a few minutes Allison called me back. In a panic, I blurted out what had happened. She said, "I'm on the way."

I called Glenn and asked him to come home immediately. He was at Home Depot picking up supplies. He dropped everything right where he was and left the store.

Sitting in the paddock, I tried to calm Molly by stroking and keeping her quiet. I held all the wounds in turn, trying to stop the bleeding. In what seemed like forever, but was only about twenty minutes, the veterinarian, some people from MuttShack with whom I had been rescuing animals, and my husband came to our aid.

A lady who works with MuttShack and specializes in pit bull rescue took Red Sam right away and later found a more suitable home for him. The last I heard, he was doing well and not showing any further signs of aggression.

While Molly was down, we cleaned and bandaged all four of her legs. Dr. Barca put in seventeen staples to hold Molly's jaw together and stitched her belly wound. Because Molly couldn't walk, we had to get her up and on to a blanket slipped underneath her. The four of us raised her, and we hobbled along to a stall in the barn.

Molly, the Survivor

Molly's wounds required intensive daily care. This was when I started to realize Molly's mettle and how smart she was. She had bandages on all four legs, top to bottom, plus her stitches and staples. When I'd clean her injuries every day, she never gave me any trouble. If it had been my wounds, I would have been kicking and screaming at someone who was cleaning them. As I did therapy on her right front leg, the one with the worst injury, I noticed it was cold at the bottom, by the ankle.

As the days went on, and Molly roamed freely in our front yard, I noticed she didn't put any weight on her right front leg. Instead, she moved the left front leg that wasn't too damaged to the middle of her body and walked on only three legs, tripod fashion. Dr. Barca's associate, Dr. Herzog, came to check Molly's leg. He expressed concerned about the cold ankle and apparent lack of circulation on the bad leg, even though most of the wounds on the other three legs, as well as her belly and jaw, were almost healed.

Another thing Molly started to do was to pick out a particular spot in the front yard where she would lie down. I looked at it and noticed that there was a dip in that spot. Because the slight incline kept her propped up, she could more easily get up and down on her three better legs. Then I noticed that her favorite spot to stand was on a little hill over a drainage pipe. She would stand with her good leg over the top of the hill and her two back legs at the bottom. This positioning pushed weight onto her back legs and gave her good front leg a break from carrying all the front weight.

As I watched Molly creatively figuring out these maneuvers, I thought, "This pony is teaching herself to survive on three legs." Thank goodness, because about three weeks after the attack, I knew we had lost the battle to keep her right front leg. During the daily therapy on the only wound that didn't heal, I felt a pop in her hoof or ankle. She reared up, shaking in pain, but was very careful not to hit or hurt me. I stroked her and asked, "Molly, what do you want me to do?"

I could hear Molly's answer in my mind. She said, "I want to survive; I want to keep going." It was as clear as if she had spoken to me.

After I bandaged her leg again, and she hobbled off, I went inside and got on the Internet. I found a guy who does equine prosthetics in Florida. He had already made a front leg prosthetic for a donkey. I thought, "It can be done!"

I started emailing people and writing, "I have this pony and I would like to get her a fake leg." Almost across the board, except for the guy in Florida, I got the answer, "No, it can't be done." I kept communicating with people and saying, "You don't understand. Molly has already taught herself to walk on three legs. She knows how to survive and she is perfectly healthy otherwise."

Dr. Barca came out and looked at Molly's bad leg. By this time it was hanging by a thread. She said, "Okay, time to put her down." I told Allison that I wanted to find a prosthesis for this brave little survivor. Allison thought I was trying to do something that would be cruel, inhumane, and impossible, and she told me so. I started crying and pleading that she didn't understand. I said, "I would never hurt Molly. She's healthy otherwise. There is a donkey. . . . We have to do it. Look at her."

Allison looked at me and then at Molly. Suddenly it seemed as if Molly must have zinged her, because Allison stopped and considered what I was saying. She said, "All right. Let's call Louisiana State University [LSU]."

After Allison called the LSU School of Veterinary Medicine, she heard the same objections she'd herself raised. The veterinarian on call spoke so fervently that Allison had to move the phone away from her ear. She closed the conversation by asking to have Dr. Rustin Moore call her. At that time, Dr. Moore was the director of the Equine Health Studies Program (EHSP) and of the LSU Equine Clinic. Beyond the fancy titles, Dr. Moore was a colleague whom Dr. Barca trusted to listen to her and give our ideas about Molly a fair hearing.

Dr. Moore called back and sounded skeptical too, but Allison and I asked that he meet the pony. Dr. Moore agreed. I knew that unless he met Molly, he couldn't know her personality and determination. I call the way she enchants people "Molly Magic."

Molly's Surgery at LSU

A day after the call to Dr. Moore, we got Molly ready for her journey to Baton Rouge. I was worried about having her in the trailer with only three good legs, so I rode in it with her. Not something a person is supposed to do, but these were exceptional circumstances. Molly aced the ride, balancing on her three good legs.

At LSU the medical staff cut off Molly's dead hoof. They rebandaged her, x-rayed the good feet, and took blood tests to see if she could make it through surgery to have the leg removed. They checked Molly for laminitis, more commonly known as "founder." When a horse isn't getting circulation to her feet or when there are other stresses on the horse, the inner bone in the hoof rotates and drops down through the sole of the hoof, which is very painful and bad for the horse. Sometimes the biggest problem with a leg injury is that the good feet go bad.

After the testing was completed, I stood by Molly's stall, waiting for results. I took Molly from her stall to the nearby patch of grass. Molly loves to eat grass. The vet student standing by her stall said, "Don't make that pony move."

I have the firm belief that one of the main reasons Molly made it was that I did not keep her stuck in a stall, where she would have lost circulation in her good legs. I gave Molly the chance to figure out what was best for her own healing. This vet student was telling me not to do what I'd done with Molly for the last three weeks, which was giving her free rein of our front yard. I said, "Get out of my way," to the startled student. Molly hobbled up front. When she saw the grass, she pulled me the rest of way toward it.

Later, I sat down with Dr. Moore and his associate. Dr. Moore said that they had no objections to doing the surgery, but this could not be a charity case. I would have to come up with $5,000 to pay for it. He explained that if at any point the procedure was going badly, I had to agree to have Molly euthanized immediately. I agreed because, of course, I had never wanted to let Molly suffer. "But," I added, "it will not go badly."

From that point on, Molly's surgery was a go. Molly had shown Dr. Moore that she had the will to survive. She had impressed him with her intelligence, sweetness, ability to deal with pain, and willingness to be handled. I had been able to assure him that I'd give her the daily care she would require.

All these factors boded well for a successful surgery. I had only one big obstacle: I was penniless after Katrina. I had been underinsured. My mobile home was totaled, and our barn needed repairs. My business was floundering. No one was doing pony rides for birthday parties since the hurricane. Through the good graces of other people, who helped us survive by donating feed and hay for my ponies, we had made it through. With no income and our reserves dwindling rapidly, I didn't know how I would pay for Molly's surgery.

I started emailing people and organizations and asking for money. The first person to respond was Jill Starr, who runs Lifesavers Wild Horse Rescue. Jill was nominated and became one of the top ten finalists for an Animal Planet Hero of the Year award in 2008. She is truly Molly's hero. At first, Jill responded by email and asked if my request was a hoax. Now we joke about that initial encounter. I wrote her back and gave her Dr. Barca's name and phone number and told Jill that the money would go straight to LSU and not be used for any other purpose. Jill called my vet and

LSU. When she got back to me, she said that she would be able to fund half the amount I needed. Eventually the Humane Society of the United States donated the other half for Molly's surgery.

We scheduled the surgery for January 16, 2006. Since this would be the Martin Luther King Jr. holiday, and the vet school was closed that day, Dr. Moore and his surgery team would be coming in on their day off to do the surgery. Because no one was around on surgery day, I was able to observe more than an owner would normally be allowed. My daughter is a registered vet tech; she filmed the whole surgery.

Dr. Moore had called everybody who had ever done this type of surgery successfully. He called orthotics and prosthetics people to make sure the stump would be cut correctly. The night before, he had performed the surgery on a cadaver. Despite being skeptical at first, this man did everything he could to make Molly's surgery a success. He became and continues to be a respected and beloved friend to Molly and me.

In the recovery stall, because horses sometimes bash themselves while trying to recover from anesthesia, they brought Molly out of it very slowly. They let me get at her head and asked me to walk her. The average horse would have probably felt the weight of a cast on her leg and freaked out. But this gorgeous little girl moved forward and calmly put her weight on the cast. She walked right off to her stall. The vets were trying to be stoic, but I could see their tears. The surgical team hugged her.

Molly stayed at LSU for four days, and then I brought her home. She learned to get up and down with that stiff cast. She stood on her hill to take the weight off her leg. After a few weeks the vets took off her cast and found pressure sores. They bandaged her and put on another cast, which stayed in place for another three weeks.

Molly's Prosthesis

Dwayne Mara of Bayou Orthotics and Prosthetics constructed Molly's prosthesis. He said we'd have to pay a hefty price tag for the custom-made device, but in the end, he never did charge us for it. Dwayne figured out how to design a prosthetic for a horse using parts that were meant for human devices. He studied how a horse moves and observed Molly's locomotion and the angulations of her leg. When he'd come out to see her, she would nicker for him. This pony knows that she and I have another friend for life in Dwayne.

Over the course of the journey with Dwayne he made five different designs. The first one was a cool, high-tech, silicone rubber rolled over Molly's stump with a screw inserted in it. She hated that one. Within less than a month Dwayne made a second, then a third that she kept for six to eight months. Her favorite has been the fourth design, which I alternate with the fifth prosthesis. A sixth is in the works.

After Molly returned home, Dr. Barca took over her care. She brought Molly to the clinic where Dwayne fitted the first prosthesis. Molly's amputation is about two inches below the knee. The prosthetic has her knee fitting into a cup-shaped opening. Keeping the joint has allowed her to have range of motion so she can bend the leg with her knee.

So now Molly had a new leg, and I was asking, "What are we going to do next?" I am a firm believer that we all have a job in life. We can all contribute to each other some way. If you smile at someone who is having a bad day, you change the human condition. My ponies have a lifetime home with me. They bring smiles to people's faces their whole working lives. They get treated very well and can retire here, playing out the rest of their days, doing nothing.

I talked with Molly and said, "I spent lot of time and energy on you. What are we going to do?" That's when I got another Molly zinger. A mental picture came clearly into my mind. The message I received was, "We're going to the children's hospital." Molly had said she wanted to bring joy and happiness to children, people with no hope, and those with disabilities.

Molly was right. The Children's Hospital of New Orleans became her first postsurgery healing success story.

Spunky Molly

At the Children's Hospital of New Orleans, there is a courtyard area where the children are brought out for recreation time.

A therapist told me that a boy who used a wheelchair and whose head violently rocked back and forth couldn't control his head motions. I sensed that he was trying to communicate. Nobody was listening, though, and it made him frustrated. The boy was pulled next to Molly, and someone took off his headgear so he could see her. The moment he saw Molly, his head stopped moving. This boy was keeping his head still so that he could look at the pony. He and Molly gazed into each other's eyes. Molly knew she shouldn't move.

Allison asked the therapist, "Can I take this boy's hand?" The therapist, still in disbelief at what was happening, nodded yes. The boy stayed completely still while looking at Molly and touched her nose with his hand. In one of those wow moments, he was communicating with her.

After the boy was wheeled back to the hospital, Allison and I started to leave. On the way to the trailer, down the pathway, Molly turned around and jerked us back in the direction where the children had been. She even passed up a patch of grass to look for the kids. And we know how Molly loves her grass! It was as if she was asking, "Where did they go?" She had been having such a good time.

In so many ways, Molly is a Katrina comeback story. Thousands of people in New Orleans view her as an inspiration. One of the first media interviews I did was with Bill Capo, New Orleans's WWL TV's *Action News* reporter. He had helped us in the past, so I called and told him Molly's story. He said he would love to do a story but was inundated with everyone needing help. We weren't sure if he'd have the time, but he came to our ranch and hung out with Molly. Of course, she worked her charm on him. Bill was relieved to be reporting a success instead of a failure. During the interview I told Bill that I think Molly is like the city of New Orleans. The city had its leg chewed off. We're not going to ever be normal. But we can come back even better.

We did many media interviews after Molly's surgery including an article for the *New York Times*, and Molly's story circled the globe. But the really exciting times were yet to come.

LSU had a symphony called *Sound* and did a presentation for their donors. Their public relations person, Ky Mortensen, put together a video about the work of the veterinary school and its horse rescue efforts after Hurricane Katrina. The last few minutes of the video were all about Molly. When Molly's segment finished, many of the stoic horse people in the audience were in tears. The video was uploaded on YouTube, and things took off for LSU and Molly after it began to circulate on the Internet.

Pam Kaster was in the audience at LSU that day and approached me about writing a children's book. By then Molly and I were going to schools and nursing homes. The author took pictures of us at these places and at the children's hospital. *Molly the Pony: A True Story* was published by LSU Press in April 2008. Photos show sick kids and caregiver adults loving Molly. The children are hanging on her neck, face, and nose. Molly did not move except to take weight off her good leg.

Fran Jurga of Hoofcare Publishing wrote an email article about Molly that went viral. Ever since, it has been a rocket ride. We now have requests from many places for Molly to visit. In addition, Fran has donated money from her sales of Pam Kaster's *Molly the Pony* children's book to benefit the foundation I formed. Kids and Ponies — Molly's Foundation is raising money to help cover the expenses of taking Molly to fulfill requests. The foundation is accepting donations for a truck and trailer to transport Molly to all who request a visit and to assist in the rescue of other retired ponies.

I took Molly to Alexandria, Louisiana, to visit a retirement community. She did great on that. We went to a therapeutic riding center in Texas. Molly and I also visited Camp Rap-A-Hope, a summer camp in Mobile, Alabama, for children and teenagers ages seven to seventeen who have cancer. One of the little girls had a clubfoot, but Molly seemed to sense that this girl was not disabled. Molly tugged the girl along in the grass, and they shared a joyful game. The little girl handed Molly to a boy in a wheelchair who didn't have much strength. Molly adjusted to him by not pulling even a little bit. Instead, she gently put her head down, and when he tugged on her rope, Molly followed him. Even people who knew nothing about horses saw how different Molly was toward the little girl and the boy in the wheelchair.

When we go to schools where children do not have physical disabilities, Molly becomes an ambassador for amputees. Other children are often afraid of amputees, because they are different. The children don't know what to do or say to someone with such a condition. They pet Molly and touch her leg. Molly is fine with being touched, so these kids are able to lose their fear and the mystery of amputees.

Molly has a lot of lessons to teach. By example, she is telling kids about the power of believing and not taking no for an answer if you know what you're trying to do is right. Molly especially shines with children who have disabilities. She is sometimes restless with other children. I can't explain how she knows the difference, but she does.

I received a letter from a woman who had become depressed over the amputation of her leg below the knee. After reading Molly's story she, too, had a prosthesis made. Three months later she sent a picture to me of herself with the new leg. She said, "If Molly can do it, so can I."

The elderly folks and people in rehabilitation centers love Molly. With pony-whispered breath she sighs hope into people. It affects them to see her and hear the story about how Molly was almost "thrown away" but now is a contributing member of society. I tell them that everyone can do something for someone else, even if it's just to put a smile on a person's face for a moment. This reminds them that they can be useful too.

I enjoy getting to know more each day about Molly's personality. She can also be quite the diva. Generally we take her leg off at night. In the morning, if she doesn't want it on, she will not cooperate. If her stump is sore, she will push the prosthesis from my hand and hobble away on three legs. If she wants it, she stands with her leg stretched out for me to put it on. In the beginning, she would sometimes use her cast as a weapon. If it was feeding time and Glenn didn't move fast enough, she would hit the side of the stall or whop Glenn with it.

The base of Molly's prosthetic uses something called a Stomper Junior that is designed for children. It has a little smiley face on it. When Molly walks in the sand, her new leg leaves the imprint of smiley faces. This hoof print is symbolic of Molly's mission. She leaves smiles behind her wherever she goes.

MEDITATION

Molly and Kaye wouldn't give up in spite of all the tragedy this brave pony endured. When have you prevailed even though those in similar circumstances might have stopped believing and hoping?

BIRTHING FROSTBITE,
THE CHRISTMAS EVE FOAL

STEVE SCHWERTFEGER, *Crystal Lake, Illinois*

On Christmas Eve in 1977, Dr. Harold Norvell, DVM, employed me to take care of fifty horses at his Twin Cedars Farm in Huntley, Illinois, a large breeding and rehabilitation farm for thoroughbred racehorses. Dr. Norvell and his wife were going away for a much-needed holiday break. Since several of the mares were pregnant, and there were so many horses, it amazed me that they trusted me, a fifteen-year-old teenager, to do this big job by myself. On the other hand, I felt upset. Because of all the chores I'd be responsible for that night, I'd have to miss some of my family's holiday party.

As I prepared each stall with a thick bedding of straw, a bucket of feed, water, and several flakes of hay, I looked out the back door and began to get a little nervous. Daylight was disappearing much too quickly. Ten horses still had to be brought inside because of their late-stage pregnancies. The horses who remained outdoors had large lean-to sheds, bedded deeply with straw, where they could go for shelter. The weather forecaster had predicted colder temperatures along with frigid high winds.

The farm consisted of four large pastures with an open, running stream flowing across the lower portions. As colder weather and nighttime approached, the horses usually stayed close to their sheds. By the time I had prepared all their stalls, it was dark. I turned on the outside floodlight, but the full moon made it easy to see outlines of horses as I approached the fields. Thankfully, the first eight animals were easy to lead inside. They always seemed to know with an uncanny accuracy when it was time to eat.

My increasingly impatient attitude became tinged with a full dose of self-pity. I approached the farthest pasture, and my thoughts turned to bemoaning the fact that I had to do this work alone on Christmas Eve. I pictured my family at home. They were no doubt enjoying good food next to a roaring fireplace. My usual feelings of holiday goodwill were being crushed by images of everyone but me having a good time.

Horses in the Snow

As I climbed over the fence, I did not see any horse silhouettes against the snowy background. After pouring the feed into several troughs, I angrily banged an empty metal feed bucket with my hand and yelled at the top of my voice, "Come on. I don't have all night. Get over here. It's time to eat." Still, there was no movement anywhere. I started walking away from the lean-to shed and then noticed a huddled group of horses standing near the bottom of the field. Muttering under my frozen breath, I walked toward them, wondering what could be so interesting that these ordinarily ravenous horses did not seem to care at all about food or what I wanted them to do.

When I drew closer to the horses, I noticed the shadow of a horse lying on the snow. Instantly I forgot how upset I felt. I dropped the empty bucket and ran the last few yards. My heart raced. My knees started to shake.

I arrived to find one of the pregnant mares lying on her left side, breathing very heavily. Her sweat had turned to steam rising from her body. Her feet paddled in the air but suddenly stopped. The mare groaned loudly. A violent shudder overtook her body.

I approached cautiously, unsure of what was happening. I noticed the mare's tail moving up and down. Kneeling down, I ran my hand over her neck. Another low, painful grunt emanated from her mouth. She looked up at me with a sense of panic and exhaustion. Relief flashed in her eyes at the realization that someone had arrived to help her.

While looking closer at her, I realized that she was in the process of giving birth in the middle of the field, with only the five other horses and me in attendance. My heart beat rapidly. Selfish feelings of my Christmas Eve being wrecked quickly evaporated. My mind raced as I tried to decide what to do next. Should I run back to the barn and call for help? I'd have to make a long trek to the farmhouse for a telephone. Or should I just do my best and help the mare right now out in the field?

As if reading my mind, the other horses moved in closer to surround the mother. I began to realize what I must do. I had bent over to look more closely at her heaving body, but now I gazed up to see every one of the horses looking at me. Silently, they seemed to ask me to help her. A great feeling of peace and a previously unknown sense of confidence overtook me. As I looked back up across the field, I knew in my heart that I had to assist the mare right then.

Giving Birth

Relying on my limited knowledge about the equine birthing process, I assessed the situation. The mare's water had already broken. I could see that the baby had started to make its way into the world. The mother began to strain again quite hard, so I removed my warm thermal gloves, knelt down, and noticed that the baby's two feet were now visible.

Gently I grabbed the tiny feet and assisted the mare's efforts to give birth by applying traction, which meant pulling on the baby as it was being born, timed with the mother's contractions. She seemed to acknowledge that the traction was helping and strained with a renewed sense of urgency.

Steve's Frostbite

After several minutes of wondering if I was doing the right thing, there was a great rush. Suddenly I lurched onto my back with a wet, newborn foal lying on top of me. I quickly stood up and cleared the fluids out the baby's nostrils, then gently gave him a slap on the behind to start his breathing. He made a very loud snort and wagged his head, coughing out the rest of the fluids. I grabbed his front feet and moved him closer to his mother's head so that she could get acquainted with the little fellow. Realizing what was in front of her, she slowly rose up. With a renewed interest in life, she vigorously licked him. He shook his head again and attempted to stand up.

The Silent Night

I sat back down again, shaken from both the cold and what I had just experienced. I was struck by the peacefulness of the scene before me. In the silence of a beautiful moonlit evening, all the horses stood and rejoiced, in an unspoken way, the birth of a new baby. I spent several minutes drinking in the scene. Slowly I began to drift back to a different type of reality. How was I was going to get the mother and baby up the field and into the barn, where they could recover in the nice, warm stall?

Standing up with a renewed sense of determination, I circled my arms around the foal. I turned uphill, concerned about the distance to the barn, which was close to a quarter-mile away. The mare stood up with great effort and nudged her baby toward the barn. The other horses followed in unison. We all headed for the distant floodlight.

Several times I lost my balance and fell, but the mare, despite her weakened state, very patiently waited for me to get up and direct her baby, who could barely walk. At this time the wind picked up, and snow blew across the empty field. The five other horses moved into a tighter group, offering us protection as we slowly moved forward.

After about thirty minutes we made it to the barn gate. I opened it and directed the baby and mother into the building. All the other horses stayed behind, knowing that their job was completed. After a few more yards, mother, foal, and I stumbled into the stall.

Finishing the Job

I shut the door, wiped my frozen hands, and clicked on the heat lamps. Then I went over to the tack room and grabbed several large towels to help wipe down the newborn foal. This really wasn't necessary, because his mother had commenced licking him. The heat from the lamps rapidly dried his trembling little body. I dressed his umbilical stump with iodine and gave him an enema to assist in the removal of the meconium. The earliest stools of an infant, meconium is composed of materials ingested while in the uterus. It must be completely passed by the end of the first few days of postpartum life.

After finishing my care of the foal and his mother, I called Dr. Norvell and explained what had transpired. He said that he would be home shortly to see how things were going. I sat in a quiet corner of the stall. I don't know what was more effective in warming me — the heat lamps or watching the mare and foal get acquainted with each other.

Later, I went outside to finish my chores, find my gloves, and feed the other horses. As I left the warmth of the barn, I noticed that the wind had died down. The sound of recorded Christmas carols from a neighboring farmer's display wafted across the fields. I listened to the words, "Silent night, holy night; all is calm; all is bright," drift through the still, cold air.

I stopped what I was doing, put down the buckets, leaned against the fence, lowered my head, and reflected on the whole evening. The words to that song had never affected me the way they did at that moment. This whole experience began to sink into my being, making me understand for the first time that the Christmas season is about assisting others rather than selfishly waiting to see what I could get. On this sacred evening, a seed had been planted in my soul, and it affected my future in a positive way that I never would have expected.

My New Kinship with the Horses

While feeding the other horses, a special sort of kinship replaced my rushed, rude, and somewhat uncaring attitude from earlier in the evening. I spoke to the horses as old friends while teasing them and providing extra hay. I appreciated the fact that they had helped me to realize what Christmas is really about. In my life I had seen several horses born, but this one was special. I started to think about the birth of Jesus and realized how precious life is, whether human or animal.

The horses followed me down the pasture. Boy, was I glad to see my gloves along with the empty feed bucket still lying there. The horses and I walked back to the barn in what seemed like one big, happy family. They thundered around, kicking their heels up as if to express their joy that everything had worked out well. The peace and goodwill I felt carried me to the barn, where the doctor now waited.

Dr. Norvell listened to my story while examining the foal and mare, taking vital signs, and a giving the baby an injection. He turned to me, smiled, and shook my hand, congratulating me on a job well done.

The foal grew up to be an adult with white tips on his ears. His owners named him Frostbite after hearing my story about the blessed evening when he came into the world.

That night affected me in a very direct and heartfelt way, and I still reflect on this truly special evening from my youth. Cradling a foal named Frostbite in my arms on the Christmas Eve he was born became one of my inspirations for growing up to become a horse rescuer. In what has become a very important aspect of my life, I now assist horses in need as a humane investigator for the Hooved Animal Rescue and Protection Society. Horse rescue often brings with it the same sort of wonder from that long-ago night. When I see the look of appreciation in the eyes of an animal who has been given another chance, I feel a sense of gratification that no amount of material things could ever replace.

MEDITATION

A teenage boy's Christmas Eve service to a horse in need inspired him to reflect on the true meaning of this sacred day. When has an animal reminded you that wonder blossoms in the giving heart?

OLD PONY PEANUT FINDS AN OLD FRIEND

COOKY McCLUNG, *Elverson, Pennsylvania*

Nobody wanted Peanut anymore.

Like the eccentric relative everyone wished would stay in the attic, the ancient ebony Dartmoor pony had become an embarrassment. A kind and sensible friend who had taught our seven children the joy of riding, little Peanut had long been outgrown by even the youngest of our brood.

"Mother, would you please get rid of this pony!" shouted my oldest son one day after retrieving the elderly equine. A neighbor had called to say she'd found Peanut sleeping on her porch. Again. "He's senile. And useless," my son stormed.

"Just like Great-Uncle Trevor," I thought instantly.

Okay, so my son might be right. Maybe Peanut had outlived his usefulness. Though my children had long since moved on to show jumping and steeple chasing, I reminded them it was this little pony who had given them the nerve to gallop across the meadow and courage to jump their first little cross-rail. They'd forgotten how quickly they had gained confidence, sitting securely on his broad little back, as he ambled safely and slowly along. They no longer dressed him up as a troll for Halloween or hitched him to their Flexible Flyer when it snowed. Despite my gentle reminders that Peanut had been a valued friend, babysitter, and teacher to them all, the pony's increasingly frequent forays into neighboring hayfields and porches continued to frustrate my offspring.

Peanut had become a crow in a barn full of peacocks, low in productivity and high in maintenance. His tiny feet grew alarmingly fast and needed frequent and pricey visits from the blacksmith. His skin sprouted strange rashes requiring exotic creams and special soft brushes. One eye had become cloudy, and he'd developed a permanent limp. Yet during Peanut's annual checkup, the veterinarian assured us that, even with his problems, the elderly pony was in very good shape for his age. In other words, there was no real reason to euthanize him. Except that the rest of my family thought he'd become inconvenient.

The pony reminded me of Great-Uncle Trevor because, while I was growing up, our large family felt much the same way about him when he began to age. Like Peanut, Great-Uncle Trevor often wandered off and forgot his way home. Dressed in peculiar clothes, he'd regularly appear at family gatherings doing or saying something so outrageous that everyone would talk about it for months.

When I was six years old, however, I thought Great-Uncle Trevor was wonderful company. On our frequent walks together, he'd allow me to talk about all the things I loved but were of no interest to the rest of my family. I vividly recall how it hurt my feelings when a relative whispered, as they often did, "I just wish Trevor would stay out of the way!"

Fortunately, with the luck of the Irish in his favor, a funny, petite widow discovered Great-Uncle Trevor. She thought his idiosyncrasies were quite marvelous. She had a comfortable pension, a lovely little cottage, and a grand passion for the man everyone wanted to be somewhere else. They married when he was eighty-one, and she had just turned seventy. For a decade more they lived happily together, though they would be forever known as the dotty duo.

But Peanut wasn't a person. He was simply a silly, undersized, old pony who continually escaped from his pasture, needed to have his food pulverized, required daily doses of medicine for his conditions, and constantly annoyed the other horses by nibbling their tails, snatching their hay, and following them everywhere.

Missing the toddlers, now grown, who had once adored him, craving no more than a kind word or an affectionate scratch, Peanut couldn't understand that he'd become too much trouble to love. Just maybe, I thought with a heavy heart, the time had finally come to send Peanut to that big pasture in the sky. I was the only one who paid him the slightest attention. Until one day in late March.

Peanut Finds a Friend

It was a spring teaser, the first morning that had dawned without snow on the ground. I sat on the porch, brushing the dogs, when I noticed a figure at the far end of the lane where Peanut's pasture ended. Peering more closely, I saw a stooped man in a black overcoat; his wispy gray hair blew in the breeze. He carried a cane in one hand and something orange in the other. Peanut held his nose as high as he could over the fence, eagerly nibbling whatever the elderly gentleman offered.

As I walked over, the man turned slowly and smiled, introducing himself as Matthew, the father of a friend who lived two farms over. He'd recently moved in with his daughter's family, he explained, and was taking a stroll to get to know the neighborhood.

"This is a very, very fine pony," said Matthew, offering Peanut the remaining carrots. "Long ago I used to ride, though not very well. I remember how I loved to wander the countryside just conversing with my horse. Would you mind if I visited this fine pony on my walks? He seems to like to listen to me, and that's so very pleasing to the soul."

I told Matthew I'd be delighted to have him converse with Peanut. "My children have all outgrown him, and I think he'd like to feel useful again."

"Yes," replied Matthew. "I think I know what you mean."

Cooky's son, Chris, and Peanut

Over the months, the fence-rail talks between Matthew and Peanut grew to lengthy conversational strolls. The old gentleman asked if he could put a leash on Peanut and take him along on his walks.

"I think he'd like that very much," I answered.

For the pony, his new friend was heaven sent. Each morning would find Peanut peering through the fence rails, waiting for his Matthew to appear for their walk. The duo sauntered slowly up and down the dusty road, both limping slightly. Peanut munched carrots, and Matthew puffed on his pipe.

They frequently stopped to converse with others who were out and about, but I'm certain their most important discussions were just between the two of them. Pointing to the odd couple, I reminded my youngsters that, human or equine, there were many ways to be useful. And I thanked the powers that be. Peanut had finally found someone who ignored appearance and oddities to see how wonderful a pony he really was.

Rain or shine, Matthew never missed a day's walk, so I feared the worst when he failed to appear one morning in late August. I was right. Peanut's friend had passed away in his sleep that night.

For the next three days the pony kept vigil, peering down the road in search of Matthew. Refusing even the succulent carrots I offered him, Peanut was simply not interested in talking to me. Then, late on the fourth day after Matthew no longer came to walk and talk with him, the old pony lay down on the warm summer grass and went to sleep forever.

I'm not sure how it works with people and animals in heaven, but if there is a God, I'll bet he's enjoying lively conversation between one very small pony and one very kind old man.

And maybe Great-Uncle Trevor.

MEDITATION

The Peanuts, Matthews, and Great-Uncle Trevors of the world may seem to outlive their usefulness. But you have found the treasures that their lives and hearts contain, haven't you?

CHAPTER TWO

Inspiring

More than fame and more than money
is the comment kind and sunny
And the hearty, warm approval of a friend.
For it gives to life a savor, and it makes you stronger, braver,
And it gives you heart and spirit to the end.

— BERTON BRALEY

SANKOFA,
THE HORSE WHO REWROTE HISTORY

MILES J. DEAN, *Piscataway, New Jersey*

In 2000, I was a fifth grade social studies teacher at a middle school in New Jersey who felt frustrated that textbooks for my students didn't include much, if anything, about my African American ancestors. Although we studied U.S. history in my classroom, I longed to incorporate the African American aspect of our country's heritage in a much larger, broader, more stimulating way.

I started planning a journey when I was fifty-eight years old that would take me on horseback more than five thousand miles across the country, through New York, New Jersey, Pennsylvania, Maryland, Washington, D.C., West Virginia, Kentucky, Tennessee, Arkansas, Texas, New Mexico, Arizona, and California. In each state I visited I would discuss the contributions of African Americans of the United States from the 1500s through the 1800s, an era when horses were the prominent means of transportation. My odyssey would draw attention to the role African Americans played in the exploration, expansion, and settlement of this country.

Prior to launching this dream trip, in 1992, I cofounded a nonprofit organization called the Black Heritage Riders (BHR); currently I am its executive director. The BHR's mission is to enrich cultural diversity, foster pride, and contribute to building character and self-esteem in African American children. We also promote educational reform in the public school system. The BHR provides presentations on the historical roles African American cowboys and cowgirls played in the western frontier.

Riding across the country on horseback would allow me to make the connection between African Americans and the horse. My vision of the project was that it would combine my affinity and love for horses and history, passion for adventure, theatrical background, and dedication to service to disadvantaged youth. I believe that a person has not only to think but also step outside the box in creative ways in order to make significant changes. I hoped to deliver a highly inspiring history lesson on horseback.

The trip, which would take nine years to plan and prepare, far exceeded my expectations of the impact it would have on the students I taught before and would teach after the trip was completed. My fifth grade classes became a major part of shaping the trip. Before I left on my journey, my students researched themes and states I would cross. During the one-year leave of absence I took from teaching, students read my commentaries and blogs and viewed video clips and photos I took along the way. They emailed me during their social studies lessons. I called the school once each week and spoke over the intercom for five minutes, giving updates about my location.

Once in progress, my dream trip fulfilled my expectations beyond students at the school where I taught as people across the country made special acknowledgment of the significance of this journey. In many towns, police escorts aided my way as crowds gathered to greet us. Horsemen and women in major cities joined and supported me in making history come alive. A gathering of people met me in Los Angeles, California, with a welcome at the Gene Autry museum. In Phoenix, Arizona, one of the city council members and a gathering of distinguished people met, congratulated me, and presented me with a city proclamation.

The *Star Ledger*, a statewide New Jersey newspaper, gave me a telephone number to call in and speak as often as I wanted during the journey, so people could listen to or download Podcasts for a program called *Where's Miles Dean?* People could also follow articles about the trip at Nj.com/news.

I spoke to thousands of school children and faculty in states we crossed about the benefits of connecting black culture to math, science, and literature. I interviewed professors at historically Black colleges and other experts along my route to gain their perspective on historical African American themes and posted a short video of these interviews on my website.

Students and teachers, government dignitaries, friends, family, and supporters, as well as millions of ordinary people followed my journey on the Internet. They learned the history of each state told from an African American viewpoint. Themes I covered included Black Conquistadors, the Revolutionary War, slavery, the abolitionist movement, the Civil War, the Reconstruction era, the Wild West, indigenous people, the Alamo, and the Buffalo Soldiers. The rich history of African Americans who used horses to explore U.S. territories and expanded, settled, and tamed the Wild, Wild West would no longer be an untold story.

I called the project "A Modern African American Pioneer" (AMAAP). But achieving my lofty goals required that I find exactly the right horse to carry me into historical and geographical times and places. I had no idea who he or she would be, until I met the incredible buckskin Arabian-Saddlebred foal Sankofa on a farm in New Jersey.

Sankofa, Horse with a Mission

In 1997, before my dream manifested, I was looking for a house to rent that had enough land to accommodate the eleven horses I owned at the time. While I was viewing a property for sale, the elderly woman who owned it asked if I'd be interested in her three-month-old horse. He had jumped a six-foot-high fence and was turning out to be too much for her to handle.

I already had an idea of riding horseback across the country when I met the woman's mischievous horse. He was a buckskin with brown tail, legs, and mane. I purchased him because of his breeding — the kind that endurance horses have — and his young age. I hoped to groom him to help me fulfill my mission. I named the horse Sankofa, which in the Ghanaian language means "to return to get it." That, of course, is exactly what I hoped Sankofa would do — retrieve an African American history and heritage.

Miles and Sankofa

It took two years to prepare Sankofa to accept me as a rider. Ron Smith, a buddy of mine who is an experienced horse handler, helped me to develop a personal relationship with the horse. I got Sankofa to the point where he would respond to verbal commands — stop, walk, and trot. Ron conditioned him using long lines. I lunged him by exercising him using a long line, called a lunge line, attached to the halter on his head and urging him to walk, trot, and canter in a circle. This helped him to become supple so he could bend his neck from left to right.

Our training led Sankofa to become very versatile. Not only could he carry a person on his back, but he could pull a wagon or cart, which I think he prefers to having somebody ride him. His heritage includes a grandfather who was a 1967 national champion horse in riding competitions. The combination of Sankofa's genetics, training, and breed turned him into an elegant and graceful showman.

Sankofa was the perfect horse in terms of temperament,

personality, fitness, and configuration. I needed to find other horses as well, so that Sankofa could alternate with different horses and rest during our journey. I rode five other horses before I found a good match in Southern Sun, a Kentucky mountain saddle horse. Blaze, a twelve-year-old palomino, was another one of the four alternate horses I rode between New York and Kentucky.

The relationship between Sankofa and me deepened throughout the training, and so did our communication. If he saw me first, he would whinny, and I'd whinny back. If I saw him first, even at a distance, I would whinny, and he'd stop whatever he was doing and whinny back. This is how we greeted each other.

Sankofa knew the importance of this quest from the beginning. I continually told him how essential he was to fulfilling my dream. He understood my rhythm but probably not my words. To prepare we trained both physically and emotionally. We didn't just get on the road and put miles in. When he was six and seven years old, we competed in twenty-five- and thirty-five-mile endurance rides. He always enjoyed being out in woods and open land.

We went through therapy sessions given by my friend Mary Ann Brewer. For these sessions I trailered Sankofa and Blaze to Mary Ann's place, where we worked on such things as respecting each other's space and listening techniques.

The Journey Begins

Sankofa grew from being my child, only three months old, to my partner. He had matured to the age of ten when we began our journey. By then, Sankofa was not only a horse I owned and loved, but also one whose opinion I respected.

This was a spiritual journey for me because it would raise awareness of the contributions of our ancestors. Their ultimate sacrifices were the reasons we African Americans are in the positions we're in now. I considered it to be an honor to be telling at least part of their story. In the African tradition we pour libation, which is the pouring of water and saying certain words in the name of ancestors who have done good deeds. Many times, libation is poured to honor the ancestors, sometimes where they met their destruction in a violent or unsavory manner. Part of my goal was to pour libation along the way, so I prepared to have this brief but meaningful ceremony performed at certain locations. Sankofa and I launched our journey by having libation poured at the African Burial Ground in Manhattan on September 22, 2007, and ended with another libation ceremony at the California African American Museum in Los Angeles eight months later.

The Stallion Sankofa

Sankofa's behavior on this trip was unlike that of any stallion I had ever known. After he had spent his first two years on the three-acre ranch in Piscataway where he grew up, he began to show rowdy stallion behavior with a mare named Chardonnay. I had to bring him to another place to keep an eye on him. I told him that if he didn't change his aggressive ways, he would not be able to stay a stallion. This warning must have had quite an effect on him, for he began to show a calmer and more eloquent demeanor.

He's a 15.1-hands stallion and full of testosterone, but during our ride he would assert himself only around other horses. If it was just the two of us on the road, and we met other people, he cooperated in a most un-stallionlike way. He'd calmly allow me to have conversations with people whether I was on his back or on the ground. At one point, three hundred screaming children rushed at us and were being pushed from behind by other children. The crowd did not stop till they were two feet away and surrounding us from every direction. Sankofa never moved a muscle or lifted his head. I think he was well aware of his role as a goodwill ambassador and accepted it like the champion that he is.

He also let me know when horses whom I had picked to partner with him were not the right ones. Even when he's being an assertive stallion, he has the kind of temperament that enables him to get along with everybody. But if Sankofa thought that a horse I wanted to serve as his alternate was going to cause a problem, he would tell me by going after the horse, making it clear that he didn't want the horse candidate for this job to be near him. This was an uncharacteristic behavior and something I'd never seen him do in the ten years I'd known him. It turned out that he was right every time. He always knew the difference between horses who were or were not good to be around.

Our Obstacles

Shortly after I began working on A Modern African American Pioneer, I was diagnosed with a brain tumor. I made the choice of treating the tumor with holistic methods and refused chemotherapy. For a couple of years, I had to focus on my life-or-death situation. I knew that the tumor could grow and cause physical difficulties.

Thoughts that I might soon be leaving this Earth served only to increase my sense of urgency, so I shortened the time frame for beginning the project. I had to set a new start date that would enable me to finish the cross-country journey before my physical issues might overtake me. The Black Heritage Riders could accept donations for funding the trip, but I wasn't able to raise money fast enough. So I decided to fund the project myself, putting more than $100,000 into it, including all my savings. Luckily I didn't lose my job but was able to take a one-year, unpaid leave of absence from my teaching position. Motivated by my passion to serve youth and humanity, I summoned the spirit and determination that propelled me to fight the nemesis of a brain tumor and fortunately to win the battle.

But there were other battles ahead when Sankofa and I got on the road. We ran across no snakes, bears, lions, or other dangerous wildlife. Our struggle was against the elements, with Mother Nature at her finest, throwing everything at us — rain, snow, desert, heat, storms, and mountains.

To accompany me, a truck pulled a horse trailer with living quarters, and an entourage of four drivers each stayed with us for one or two months. They flew in and out of the locations where we connected. My supporters believed in what I was doing and gave up their time. Without their help I could not have succeeded at the comfort level in which we traveled nor documented it so well. The drivers took care of the horses, allowing me to focus on riding and then resting. I also had an official still and video photographer. I kept in touch with my support team by cell phone and at times had short wave radio contact with the driver who drove ten miles ahead or behind me to avoid having the huge trailer hold up traffic.

After only two weeks into the journey, I felt concerned when Sankofa suffered an injury. He wore easy boots, a sort of horse sneaker, but the two back shoes had been torn off midway into a very rocky trail ride we had taken with cowboys in Maryland. Outside Kentucky, due to the prior barefoot condition, an abscess formed on his foot. We got medical attention for it, and everything seemed fine. Then a second abscess appeared on the other hind foot, and Sankofa had to be treated and healed, costing $1,000 in veterinarian bills. All of this took Sankofa out of action for days. But he recovered, determined and focused on completing his mission.

Sankofa's Dedication and Loyalty

It was important for me to pour a libation over the Arkansas River on the Arkansas–Texas Bridge. Many African Americans had lost their lives in that river during the 250 years when slavery was the rule of the land. Some were violently drowned and others took their own lives so as to not be subjected to living as animals. Still others died trying to escape slavery.

Sankofa is typically very skeptical about walking alongside eighteen-wheeler trucks, whether they're standing still or moving. He hesitates passing those vehicles or having them pass him. On the long and high Arkansas–Texas Bridge, eighteen-wheelers were flying by at sixty miles per hour. I wanted to pour libation from the bridge, but the trucks were making Sankofa nervous. His anxiety filtered to me, and I questioned whether we could safely stop in the middle. I noticed that the railing that would prevent cars from plunging into the river was not very high. I decided I couldn't risk pouring the libation in that spot, although I really wanted to do so.

It was almost as though Sankofa sensed that this significant ceremony needed to happen. When we got to the middle of the bridge, he lessened his nervous reaction and became calmer, allowing a beautiful moment of quiet peace. I took out the bottle of water, poured the libation, and said a few words of respect for the deceased ancestors, and we continued crossing the bridge. Sankofa had allowed the libation to be performed and was willing to cooperate in spite of his anxiety.

Our Greatest Obstacles and Sankofa's Wisdom

The only time I wondered about how long Sankofa and I could endure the journey was when we crossed the immense and great state of Texas. At more than seven hundred miles wide it took more than twenty days to cross it, compared to only five days to cross New Mexico. I enjoyed the scenery, although the plains became monotonous. As if to spark my interest, Texas gave me its toughest welcome with wind, rain, snow, heat, cold, and dust. I kept asking myself, "When will I be through Texas?" In El Paso at the Senora Ranch, I took a four-day break. After moving on into New Mexico, I told a reporter for the *Star Ledger*, who had called for an update, that traveling through Texas had hurt my kidney and back and tired my horses. Even though it had been difficult for me to step into the saddle and ride again, I had pushed on, amazed at what the mind can tell the body to do. The best part of the journey was that I had Sankofa as my partner. I often asked his advice when we were faced with obstacles. For example, when we were crossing the mountains and deserts in California, I always tried to find paths that would keep me as close as possible to the highway where my support vehicle was located. Sometimes I had to ride down into an arroyo because the mountain range was too high to climb. But in following the arroyo on one particular day, I noticed it kept taking me farther away. I decided to climb the mountain and get to the other side, which would bring us closer to the highway.

Sankofa had a different opinion. A quarter-way up the mountain he didn't want to continue, but I wasn't listening. I kept urging him to go on. He did. When we got halfway to the top, he stopped and refused to move. Then I knew something was wrong, so I looked behind me and saw what we had climbed. When I realized how treacherous this path had been, I was not impressed with myself or pleased with what I had done.

I dismounted and decided to go back. It was very dangerous to descend the same way we had climbed up. I feared for the safety of both of us. I had no choice but to continue climbing on foot at an angle since we couldn't walk straight up. We got to the top of the mountain range eventually. I realized that Sankofa had been warning me the whole time, "You don't want to do this." And he was right. It took about an hour before we could get off the top of that mountain range. We had to cross into a connected mountain range that would allow us to descend a less steep slope to the highway. This was the last time I did not listen to Sankofa's advice.

Along the route I was asked a couple of times if there was ever a time when I doubted that we would finish. Even though Texas had been rough, my answer was always, "No, I never doubted. And neither did Sankofa." We had both made a commitment to the mission of honoring my ancestors. Every day, I plotted out my trail for the next day and took stock of where I had already traveled. Sankofa and I took one mile at a time. It wasn't until I drove back home in a vehicle and looked out the window that I realized the magnitude of what we had accomplished. If I had not been using tunnel vision, never being distracted by things outside my plan, I may not have accomplished the goal.

End of the Journey

We averaged about twenty miles a day, depending upon the weather, terrain, and condition the horses and I were in. There were days when we went up to forty-six miles. I had calculated that the trip would take less than six months and planned on finishing in February during Black History Month. But our quest ended on April 1, 2008, at a most appropriate place, the California African American Museum (CAAM) in Los Angeles.

People cautioned us that the toughest part of this journey would be negotiating through Los Angeles. But with the help of a couple of local cowboys led by Robert Terrell, Sankofa and I were able to avoid injury in traffic. Robert also helped me make contact with CAAM.

Our attempts to arrange for the final libation ceremony at CAMM had eluded us for the last few days of the journey, but at the last minute we received permission from the museum director to come on to the grounds for our closing celebration. Local children, the cowboys and cowgirls who escorted me into a number of cities, and my entourage of driver and photographer/cameraman were in attendance. The ceremony included libations poured for the ancestors by Kamau Khalfani, host of *Under the Learning Tree* on New York's WBAI radio.

On May 16, 2008, our adventure came full circle when Sankofa and I rode to Chancellor Avenue School in Newark, New Jersey, where I teach.

Sankofa and I still talk to each other every day. We've gained even more respect and love for one another. He knows me well, so probably in his mind he's preparing for the next adventure.

E. Etherlbert Miller, director and literary activist at the African American Resource Center at Howard University, said about A Modern African American Pioneer, "Young African American kids fortunate to see Miles Dean might just go to bed with new possibilities in their heads. A black man on a horse in the twenty-first century might just be a good omen. . . . His desire to connect to the Black experience seems to be rooted in his passion to remind us that America can be America again."

As a teacher and an African American man who believes that he is a role model to younger children, I live by this philosophy: My purpose in life is to inspire, motivate, and save one child; one man — one child. I'm not looking to save the world. If I help one child in my lifetime, I've done my job. This philosophy keeps my frustration and anxiety level down and allows me to function at a very high level. I'm hoping that I've touched more than one child, but if I positively influenced one, the entire journey was worth it.

Some would say I'm dedicated and some would say, "You're a fool." All we have in life are our dreams that make us achieve. Sometimes we hold on to and sometimes we lose the dream. If I can inspire someone to fulfill a lifelong dream, it's a good thing.

MEDITATION

The outstanding relationship between Miles and Sankofa brought them into harmony for the greater good. When have you transcended all you thought was possible with the help of a horse?

TOOK INSPIRED ME TO RESCUE MORGANS

KIMBERLY BLOSS, *West Monroe, New York*

Leaning against the white three-rail fence at Harmony Riders Association, I swatted mindlessly at a mosquito and watched my summertime friends practice the maneuvers I knew by heart. Harmony Riders Association is a riding club in scenic Parish, New York, that hosts horse shows, trail rides, and clinics. At age fifteen, I was usually the one out in front barking orders, correcting spacing, and perfecting lines. Each summer we worked hard to create the finest looking horse-and-rider drill team in New York State and always reached for the championship title.

As my friends completed the ten-minute routine, the horses and riders came to rest at the fence to my right. Mothers strode with water bottles toward dusty children, whose horses nosed around for treats in parents' pockets. My best friend, Jill, squeezed the sides of her white gelding, Sinarie-O, until he ambled toward me. I looked up as she neared me, dropped her reins, and slid down off her horse. After climbing over the fence Jill hugged me, and we both started to cry. "I'm really sorry," she said. "We're all really sorry." Through the prism of my tears, I saw the rest of the team watching. Most of them reached a hand up to wipe their eyes. One younger boy rode away so that no one could see his eyes fill up.

It had been three days since my sixteen-year-old chestnut-colored half-Arabian gelding, Whiskey, had come down with colic. We'd had to humanely euthanize him. My friends and I were still in shock over his loss.

In the weeks that followed Whiskey's death, I felt empty. Even with five other horses in the barn, I had no desire to ride. Whiskey had been challenging to ride because he was a stocky, forward-moving freight train of a horse. I had so much love for him that my heart was stretched out and couldn't return to its normal shape. Now, I'd lost all interest for the very thing I'd done since before I could walk. I couldn't imagine loving any horse the way I'd loved Whiskey or ever again risking the pain of losing another horse.

I finished that summer riding a handful of different horses. For competition, I borrowed Holly Might, a friend's American paint horse mare. She was a beautiful paint show horse with chestnut and white spots who knew her job. We had a flawless performance that year at the state fair. When the judges announced our county as the champions, I burst into tears. I'd made a promise to Whiskey to finish the season for him and felt like the team had put in their best performance in his honor.

Took Is No Whiskey

It came time for the annual Harmony Riders Association trail ride in the fall, and I didn't want to go. But all my summertime friends were participating, and Jill insisted that I couldn't miss it. When I told my mother that she would be trucking my twenty-four-year-old quarter horse mare, Susie, to Harmony for the trail ride, she said, "You'll be walking there alone. That mare is out of shape and going blind. There's no way you're taking her."

My mother offered an alternative: "Why don't you take Took?" she asked. Jaklee Mr. T, otherwise known around the barn as Took, was the Morgan gelding who had recently become ours. He had been boarded with us when his owner fell on hard times and could no longer afford to pay his expenses. Since Took was already living with us, and his owner could see the excellent care he was receiving, she signed him over to us, knowing that he'd have a good home.

I wasn't so sure about this idea. Took was a wild thing, and his reputation preceded him. His previous owner had told us that when Took was born, they called him T because of the shape of a defined white star on his forehead. She had met T when he was six months old and had instantly fallen in love with his plucky character. She traded a fully trained Morgan gelding plus enough money to make up the difference in the asking price, convinced that T would be the finest show horse there ever was. When she and her trainer started

Kimberly's Took

to work with T, he showed them that he was quite capable of thinking for himself and far too smart to be told what to do. Within his first year, the owner was told that she really got "took" on the deal. The name Took stuck.

Whiskey had been skittish, flighty, and fast, but I had adjusted to his character quirks. Took appeared to be brave and stubborn, calculating, and powerful. Yet I had to admit he had a fierce beauty. His coat was a liquid chocolate color with rust highlights that glinted in the sun. His eyes were large and expressive. He was only about 15 hands tall with solid bone in his leg and defined muscles in his neck, chest, and down his haunches, which made him appear much larger than he was. He used those muscles to curl up like a spring and propel himself in any direction he chose. His robust strength terrified me.

As the days went by, my mother continued to insist that I ride Took on the trail. My riding instructor agreed with her. It seemed to me that neither of them liked me very much.

Finally I buckled under their pressure. I loaded that hot-blooded Morgan onto the trailer, and we set off for Harmony. I dreaded our arrival. I pondered the concept of prayer, hoping that might keep me from breaking my neck. I began to shake from the inside.

We pulled in next to the barn that stabled horses during shows. I heard a sharp, insistent pounding from the bowels of our steel trailer. As we lowered the trailer ramp, the pounding quit. My mother unloaded Took and handed the lead rope to me. Expecting some sort of electric shock, as if I'd grabbed a hot wire, I thought this gelding would explode with fury. Instead, he became very still. Then he arched his neck and puffed up, like Morgans do, making his liver-chestnut body appear at least two inches taller. His thick, wavy mane blew away from his neck and flagged in the breeze. He drank in the scents of Harmony with flared nostrils and wide eyes. It was the first time I remember reading his thoughts. The sentence, "This is all mine," came drifting into my mind. In the next instant he dropped his head, and the magic moment ended. Took returned to being just a brown gelding standing next to a trailer. But he had transformed me into a girl about to fall in love again.

We Become a Team

Although Took had stolen my heart during the experience at Harmony, for a while afterward we were only as stable as a pyromaniac sitting on a powder keg. Both of us headstrong when we rode, he demanded to have his way and I demanded to have mine. Whenever I cued him to canter, he would throw a swift buck punctuated by a defiant squeal. When I pointed him at a little fence to jump and rode him toward it, as if I were the one in charge of moving each of his hooves for him, he would veer off at the last minute. Then he would canter through the rest of the pasture like he didn't have a care in the world.

After about a month of fighting with Took and getting nowhere, I started listening to him. I found that if I asked him to do something instead of demanding, he complied. I also noticed that if allowed to pick his own way down a trail or around obstacles, he always chose the safest route. Little by little, I started to trust him with my life. Took noticed the difference in me too and began to respond to it. He would dance in his stall when he saw me coming or nuzzle me when I entered it.

For two years, Took became one half of the lead pair in the Oswego County 4-H Horse Drill Team. We rode trails and competed at local shows in hunter under saddle classes, in which the rider uses only English tack and rides in a hunt seat saddle without the horse doing any jumps. Slowly I embraced Took's robust love of life instead of being frightened by his energy. His ample curiosity became entertaining.

No small animal in the pasture was safe from his inquisitive, probing muzzle. Time and time again, in situations that most horses would shy away from — a plastic bag on the ground, a rolled-up snow fence, snakes speeding along through the grass — Took would pause to process what he was seeing and then boldly place himself directly in the middle or on top of whatever had caught his attention. He was careful on trail, making sure he trotted through trees, leaving enough space for my knees. I also began to notice that when something fascinated him, he would take a moment to contemplate it. Then he would wait for a response from me that showed I knew what was going on or what lay ahead. In a split second I would relax into the saddle, and Took would know that he could proceed. We moved as a unit, as one entity. He wasn't thinking only for himself anymore; he was thinking for both of us.

When my friend Tammy first met Took she was awestruck. She marveled at the way his mane waved behind him as he sprinted through the knee-high grass with his eyes wild and nose snorting, running for the pure joy of it. His exuberance took Tammy's breath away on a fine upstate New York summer afternoon. The sight was only slightly marred by the fact that he broke away from me in an open field. My lunge line, a long rope used for groundwork that attaches to the halter and makes the horse move around in circles, flagged out behind him, giving a show of its own. It looked like a dancing kite string on a kite that was floating away.

That afternoon was typical for Took. He had been brilliant to watch, running in the summer sun. After his moment was over, he came trotting back to me. This flamboyant display had been his way of telling me, once again, how much he hated lunging on a line. His eyes sparkled mischievously, but he had meant no harm.

My sophomore year in college, Took came to school with me, and I boarded him at a nearby stable. We spent many chilly autumn evenings in the indoor ring, with me riding bareback on him to stay warm.

Sunny autumn days saw us lounging in a sprawling green pasture with me sitting on a blanket reading a textbook while Took ate ten-foot circles around me. Periodically he'd stick his nose in my open book and nuzzle the pages to see if I was paying attention to my studies. He was very subtle in his circles, but I watched him keep one eye on the other two horses in the pasture. His circles always kept Took between the other horses and me. If he thought my safety was at stake, he protected me and saw it as a very serious job. Eventually, he began this behavior with people too. If he didn't care for whoever I was talking to, he would casually wedge his big brown chest between the person and me.

During my junior year of college, Took moved to Las Vegas with my parents. I followed two years later. The desert at dawn became our playground. I would ride him bareback amid the washes and tumbleweed. Our time in Las Vegas brought about a completely new version of us as a team. I trusted him completely to keep us safe; we spent the majority of our time riding with only a halter and lead ropes.

I moved back to upstate New York in fall 2001. Took followed me there in spring 2002. He was radiant once again. The moisture in the air and green grass agreed with him. I rode him bareback on trails. We competed in team penning with my best friend, Jill, and her nephew, Travis. The three of us rode into a group of cows and worked together to separate three specific cows from the herd in as little time as possible. We barrel-raced and weaved around poles for fun. We camped and rode under the stars at midnight. He loved it all.

Took's Farm

In 2004, my mother and I bought a farm in upstate New York that Took could call his own. He had his choice of pastures, pasture mates, and stalls in the barn. We purchased the farm with the intention of bringing only our four horses home, but within six months, we'd added Gabe, Tia, and Rippy, three more Morgans who had been starving in a dilapidated barn. Then we added a grade Morgan mare named Wilma — a grade Morgan is one without registration papers and who is considered to not have the phenotype accepted as Morgan standard for the breed — out of the Pennsylvania slaughter auctions. Wilma was fat and green broke, meaning her level of training was unknown. This made her a bargain for the kill buyers who purchase horses for human consumption. Since they get paid by the pound for a horse, Wilma's weight would have brought them more money at the slaughterhouse. Because she was green broke, the kill buyers wouldn't have had to bid against horsemen who look for a horse who doesn't require training for their purposes. We believed Wilma deserved a shot at a useful, happy life, so we built another stall just for her.

After eighteen years of traveling across the country, turning barrels, chasing cows, showing hunt-seat and riding trails, I lost Took on November 26, 2007, at the age of twenty-three, when he had a freak pasture accident that resulted in an untreatable fractured femur. He spent his final hours as stoic as always, refusing to show any pain. Toward the end he would shove his head into my chest and throw me out of the stall. I believe, since he did this to no one else, that Took knew how much it hurt me to know he was suffering. When the vet administered the euthanasia drugs, and Took's legs gave way, he fought to keep his heart pumping and stay, for no one could protect me like he could. He is buried at the top of the driveway, on his farm, near the barn. His gravesite reminds me every day of his role in leading me to my life's calling.

Took had been my heart-horse. He'd taught me to fight for what I love and protect it. Without him I had no safe haven, no center. I spent a month passing his stall every day, staring into the emptiness. After that first month, I could no longer look at the space where he once had lived. I wanted to walk away from the farm and horses. I felt as badly as when I had lost Whiskey all those years ago, only this was ten times worse. Yet I knew Took would not have wanted me to let an open stall stay empty when other horses have no home. If he could no longer have the soft bedding, warm meals, and happiness that pulses through my barn, he would want someone else to enjoy it. And besides, he always hated to see me sad.

So Took became my inspiration to rescue as many Morgans as possible, especially the older ones who tend to slip through the cracks. I brought Buster home. He's an older black Percheron gelding with distinguished streaks of gray through his face. Buster had worked for the Amish his whole life and was then sent to a meat auction. He acts as an ambassador for the farm and a first horse for my friend Jeb, who is a beginning rider. Buster shows people not only how to ride horses but also how to understand and love them. He has kind eyes that speak of intelligence and is very tolerant of people just learning the art of how to care for a horse. He stretches his neck up as far as it will go and wiggles his lips when the person who is brushing hits the itchy spot on his withers. Buster stands perfectly still, never biting or kicking if a brush slips and knocks him in the leg or if a rider doesn't know how to swing his leg all the way over Buster's back.

Rounding out my stalls is TC, a twenty-seven-year-old Morgan gelding who is healthy and happy but needed a place to call his own. He is fiery, personable, and displays all of the entertaining character traits of a Morgan, such as confidence and curiosity. TC also seems to understand that it is his job to educate people about horses and Morgans in particular. He dutifully raises his hooves so that youngsters can learn how to hold and clean them. He displays quiet patience when a new person fumbles with the clasps on a blanket. He keeps his ears up, and when the new horse person is done with the task, he reaches around to give him or her a little nudge, as if to say, "Good job."

We all greatly miss Took at the farm, but his strength lives on. He is the backbone, the reason for the farm's existence. First it was a home for him and now it is his final resting place. Always this is a place of freedom. Eighteen years ago, we brought Took in, knowing little of Morgans. Now our stalls bloom with them. He is the inspiration that feeds the farm and makes it a safe haven for Morgans in need.

Although I will never have another horse own my heart as Took did, because of his love, courage, and protectiveness, my mother and I protect Morgans who have fallen through the cracks and are run through auctions or are down on their luck. Perhaps we are saving someone else's future best friend.

MEDITATION

Took inspired Kimberly and her mother to rescue Morgans and other horses. Has a horse's generous spirit instilled in you the courage and will to protect others?

FINDING MY PASSIONATE PURPOSE WITH SPRING THAW

❦

CHRISTIANNA E. CAPRA, *New York, New York*

I have been horse-crazed since I was two years old. It wasn't until adulthood, though, that I found a horse named Spring Thaw who would lead me to my life's calling.

My family couldn't afford a horse, so when I was young, I became one. I walked diligently on all fours and made my relatives hand-feed me. My mom involuntarily loaned me her hairpieces for a tail. As I grew past toddler age, we lived in the Rocky Mountains of Colorado, so I tormented my mom to make friends with our neighbors who had horses. I became a helpful "barn rat" just to be around horses and earn an occasional ride. I was always just as happy to groom, care for, and be with the horses as I was to ride them.

After I turned six, we moved to Seattle, and I had to find new horse-loving friends. Every day I wished for a horse of my own. When I was eleven years old, my dream came true. My parents purchased a horse for me, but in order to keep her I got a paper route, cleaned a doctor's office, and worked at the barn. Life was perfect when I finally had my own horse, Lochi's Cin Cinnamon, or Cin for short, a 14.3-hand Appaloosa quarter horse mare who led the way for a girl to become a young woman. She came with tack, but we rarely used it. Instead we spent most of our time riding bareback in the woods and fields, swimming in the lake, and even a taking a forbidden jaunt across a golf course. We would frequently make a pit stop at McDonald's on the way home, because Cin loved French fries, and the staff was always excited to see her at the window. I had to pay for my food, but Cin's fries were always free.

After Cin and I had spent a blissful couple of years together, Mount St. Helens erupted ash all over the Northwest and compounded a respiratory illness, a temporary infection curable with antibiotics, that Cin already had. The illness turned into a chronic respiratory disease that burst several air sacks in her lung and eventually ended Cin's life when I was thirteen. After I lost Cin, my parents divorced, and the next couple of years were a confusing, frustrating time for me. A rage grew within me as I left my father's house to live with my mom and stepfather. In the summer of my junior year in high school, I was told we were moving to New York City. I didn't want to move. I had friends, and the thought of starting all over and being the new kid in New York City scared me. Plus there would be no horses there, right? Reluctantly, in 1984, at age sixteen, I moved from Seattle to New York City.

I knew I could not do just a little bit with horses — for me it had to be all or nothing — so this cross-country move started my ten-year hiatus away from them. I finished high school and college without horses as a physical part of my life. In 1990 I graduated from Marymount Manhattan College on the national dean's list with a BFA in theater arts. I began an onslaught of auditions while waiting on countless tables. As time went on I began to realize that deep within, some piece of me was missing or lost. One day I came across a photo of Cin and me, which immediately brought tears streaming down my face. This reaction made me realize that without doubt or further delay, I needed to rekindle my relationship with horses.

Meeting Spring Thaw

On Easter Eve in 1995, I wandered around my neighborhood and found myself on the Upper West Side of Manhattan. The thought struck that I must be near Claremont Riding Academy, where anyone could rent a horse to ride in Central Park. I decided to try to find it. My soul was hungry to be with horses again, so I figured that if I could just see or even smell a horse, this alone would serve as a spiritual meal.

When I arrived at Claremont, on West 89th Street, the barn had closed for the day, but there was a loose horse in the tiny arena, probably turned out to get exercise. I noticed a sign in the window that said, "Help Wanted. Part-time Groom Needed Weekends."

"Hey," I thought, "this is a way for me to be around horses again and even get paid for it." I applied and got hired for the job. I went to work by the following weekend, realizing that the $4 an hour would cover a sandwich and the subway ride. But the important payment would be that I'd spend my day surrounded by approximately sixty horses. A perk of this job was that I could ride them on Mondays.

Over the next six to eight months, I worked at Claremont every weekend. I rode just about every horse in the barn. One day, I rode a horse named Spring Thaw, a 16.1-hand Appaloosa and Thoroughbred-cross gelding. His left eye was a striking blue color, and the right one was light brown. He had a deep red coat that glistened like copper in the sun, complemented by two white socks and a white blanket with red spots over his hindquarters. His outstanding physicality was served up alongside quite a personality. Spring Thaw had a bit of a bratty reputation with the staff. He hadn't passed the tests to give lessons in the tiny arena for children or for jumping. He could go to Central Park with riders. Later, I learned that this was part of his shrewd master plan to avoid working twelve- to fourteen-hour days.

When I had my first opportunity to ride Spring Thaw, I was warned to not canter him in the park. If he did canter, I should beware of a maneuver he had perfected. He would drop his shoulder and then spin 180 degrees in order to safely remove his rider. With the rider gone, he could graze for a while and then cross four blocks of city traffic, trotting by himself back to the barn.

Indeed, on our first ride Spring Thaw tried to canter and remove me, but I did not fall. From that point on, we formed a quirky friendship. I think that we both realized that we could get along with each other. Spring had a sense of humor and a humanlike quality in the way he'd look at a person. Sometimes it seemed that he knew what I was thinking and wanted me to be aware of it. We had fun together; it reminded me of the enjoyable times I'd spent with Cin. Spring Thaw soon became my favorite horse to ride, as we regularly strayed from the bridle trails and explored the rest of Central Park.

Christianna and Spring Thaw

I came to know more about Spring Thaw as we spent time together. He had been at Claremont for only about six months when I met him. He was young, eight or nine years old. He was ornery and a little bossy. Being slightly mischievous, he'd never be mean but always managed to keep me alert and often made me laugh out loud.

I concluded that Spring Thaw had been beaten or mistreated in his past. If I made sudden movements near his face, he quickly shrank away as if he feared being hit in the head. He became very frightened of anyone coming into his stall with a pitchfork. He also was terrified of black garbage bags. I later learned that Spring Thaw was a "ridge-ling," which means that he was a fully developed stallion before he had been gelded. This explained his oral fixations and occasional studlike behavior. But it also contributed to his great survivor instincts and true stoic presence with regard to pain or suffering.

There were signs that he was starting to reach out to me emotionally. He'd lick my arms when I was in his six-by-eight-foot stall. Then he'd block the door if I tried to leave. He didn't do these things with anyone else. I could feel a presence whenever I was around him. It was as if he was in tune with a part of me that housed my deepest desires and fears. I felt a strong sense of security and peace when we were together and even if I only thought of him.

Spring Thaw Becomes Mine

One day I arrived at the barn and heard the owner talking about liability and saying he had to get rid of that horse. I asked whom he was talking about. It was Spring Thaw. He had once again left a rider in the park somewhere, grazed on the public lawns, covered four blocks of busy traffic, and returned, sans rider, to the barn. Only this time, he had company after convincing another horse named Milky Way that running away was the cool thing to do. So both horses had traveled among the taxicabs and fire trucks, landing the attention of a radio news reporter who shared the story with the rest of New York City. The unwanted publicity prompted Spring Thaw to get his walking papers from Claremont.

"What will happen to him?" I asked. "Where will he go?" The owner said that he would ship Spring Thaw to a horse dealer on Long Island. From there I assumed, a family, another barn, or worst of all, a horsemeat buyer could purchase him.

I ran home, feeling panicked. Somehow I had to find a way to save Spring Thaw. My boyfriend, Michael, asked, "Why don't you take him? You talk about him all the time and you seem to like him a lot. They will probably give you a deal."

I thought this was a crazy idea. I know what a commitment is required to have a horse. It's a lot of responsibility, and especially difficult since I live in the city.

Within two days the owner and I had worked out a payment plan. In six months Michael and I had paid for Spring Thaw. We hunted for a farm in New York State or New Jersey that had open fields and grass so that Spring Thaw could live a life with more freedom. I wasn't totally sure why I was getting a horse at that point in my life. I thought, "What if I can't take care of him? I can hardly take care of myself." But there remained a quiet, persistent voice inside me that kept saying it would end up okay and that this was the thing to do.

Claremont is now closed. In many ways I believe that is a good thing. Although a landmark building, serving as the oldest working livery stable on the East Coast, it looked every bit its age. While it served as some semblance of a home and the horses were fed and watered, they were boarded in dark, narrow stalls. They didn't usually get to run in a field or eat grass. Only Spring Thaw had devised a way to graze in Central Park when he threw off riders.

I found a barn in Warwick, New York, and brought Spring Thaw there to live. The day I turned him loose in a field, he ran around and around with his head high and his tail up; he whinnied and snorted with sweat running from his face. The sight brought tears to my eyes. After stopping he came to me and softly put his nose on my shoulder. I looked into his eyes and saw a calmness that had not been there before and felt him say, "Thank you."

Over the next ten years Spring Thaw and I became the best of friends. We competed in lower-level eventing for four years. Eventing is an equestrian sport that resembles a triathlon, combining a total score from three separate phases — dressage, cross-country jumping, and stadium jumping. We struggled a bit with the dressage, had a blast on cross-country, and generally went clear on the stadium jumping. We won a few of our events and placed in many others. But mainly Spring Thaw was teaching me to trust him and myself.

Spring Thaw demonstrated an unusual intelligence. One morning, the barn manager came in and found the barn an absolute mess, with things strewn all over the place. Most of the stall doors were open and nearly all the horses were loose outside the barn and grazing, except for Spring Thaw. He stood quietly in his stall with his door ajar and the most innocent look on his face as if to say, "What? Do you think I had something to do with this?" We later caught him in the act of setting himself free and concluded that, yes, that incident had been entirely his doing. This new trick earned Spring Thaw an extra security clip on his stall door.

Ultimately this horse is my friend and teacher. From him I have learned patience, confidence, trust, spontaneity, perseverance, true unconditional love, and that nothing beats a sense of humor. I know that Spring Thaw has had an effect on others as well. I would often find notes taped to his stall door from complete strangers, thanking me for my horse entertaining their son or daughter or dog.

Spring Thaw has helped me through some of the toughest times and decisions, mainly by just being the one constant I could count on. Right around the time that he came into my life at Claremont, I had lost a pregnancy. As I look back on that difficult time, I realize that Spring Thaw in many ways became my son, teaching me responsibility, faith, and tenacity. After the stable closed for the night, Spring Thaw offered me great comfort when we were alone. One time I started to cry about the miscarriage, and he wrapped his head and neck around my torso, giving me a horse hug. I felt so much warmth and love at that moment. Through job losses and very uncertain times along with a search to find my calling in life, no matter what happened, he has consistently been there to frisk me for a carrot, make me laugh, and keep me engaged in the present moment.

Illness Brought Change

In late 2004, Spring Thaw contracted Lyme disease. He started acting old, and I noticed his growing apathy about things that he normally loved. He probably had suffered from Lyme disease for a long time until he couldn't hide it anymore. At this point I retired him from competing and riding. This was a little sad for me, but as I witnessed his deterioration, I wanted only for him to get well.

We ran through three courses of drug treatments, including a twenty-one-day IV treatment, which started to tax his kidneys and had to be stopped. We tried varied drug dosages over more than two years. After each treatment we would rest his body from the drugs and use these breaks to see if the treatments had worked. Each time the Lyme disease roared back worse than it had been before.

I began to despair but couldn't stand the thought of losing my dear friend. Then in 2007, a colleague introduced me to a very special veterinarian, Judith M. Shoemaker, DVM, who is internationally known for her successes in restoring horses' health. She includes alternative methods and holistic therapies in her practice. Dr. Shoemaker had seen a scenario like Spring Thaw's before, and she classified him as both chronic and drug-resistant for Lyme. She wanted to put him on a regimen of herbs, acupuncture, and oxygen, or ozone, therapies. At this point I had nothing more to lose and agreed to her suggestions. For the next nine months I witnessed a steady and noticeable improvement in Spring Thaw. Little by little, my boy was finding his way back to me.

As of October 2008, I am very relieved and happy to say that Spring Thaw is well and back 100 percent to his mischievous self. He is estimated to be twenty-two years old but still insists that age is only a number. He spends his days grazing next to an eighteen-year-old Arabian and runs, rears, and plays with the younger horses in the fields where he lives. His energy has returned along with his zest for life and fun attitude.

Spring Thaw knows he is loved and cherished. I ride him now for enjoyment, mostly bareback, in the woods and trails. If he wants to canter, I let him and soak it up as a gift. For his retirement I made a deal with him — I decide the path we travel, and he decides the pace. Every now and then, he takes off and throws a few bucks in for good measure to keep me on my toes. Or maybe he's just reminding me that he isn't finished with life yet. We have a second chance together, and we're loving it.

Spring Thaw Led Me to a New Career

I have always wanted to create a career with horses but being a trainer, professional rider, or veterinarian didn't appeal to me. During our therapy with Dr. Shoemaker, she recommended to me, "Eagala.org [Equine Assisted Growth and Learning Association]. Check it out. This horse would be a brilliant equine-assisted psychotherapy [EAP] horse."

EAP is a form of emotional balance treatment using three treatment team members to help people with emotional problems, imbalances, and healing. It can successfully treat addiction problems, eating disorders, behavioral and performance problems, at-risk youth, families and couples in need of therapy, and so much more. The team consists of a credentialed mental health professional, who also becomes EAGALA certified; an equine specialist, who works with the horses; and the therapy horses. All the therapy work is done on the ground with no riding involved. The horses are generally loose and interact with clients on their own herd terms. The horses are free to mirror emotional states and use nonverbal metaphors to illustrate issues for the treatment team to address.

Following Dr. Shoemaker's advice, I have become an EAGALA-certified equine specialist as part of the EAP treatment team.

On this journey, I have found my spirit guide in Spring Thaw. Through him I have discovered my life's work, or my passionate purpose. Spring Thaw has a tremendous gift for this therapy work in that he is extremely sensitive to the energy around him. When given the freedom to express himself, he won't let clients hide behind facades or masks. He gently helps them to see what he sees and begin their self-healing. He has never been wrong and never lies. He may shake things up a bit but will offer a soft place to land.

Now I see that Spring Thaw's illness caused us to shift gears. It enabled me to find EAGALA and the path for the rest of my life. This is my way of serving others while working with horses. How fortunate I am to be able to do EAGALA with my truest and best friend as my partner and master teacher.

I am so very grateful for the day that I wandered into Claremont and met Spring Thaw. It seems that no matter where we are — in the midst of New York City traffic or lost at dusk in the woods — he always knows how to get us home. He remains the one truth I can believe in.

MEDITATION

Spring Thaw made it clear to Christianna that he possessed the will to live and his life has purpose. What are the signs that you are longing to fulfill your passionate purpose?

AVENGER — DESTINY COMES FULL CIRCLE

KIM MCELROY, *Kingston, Washington*

On January 3, 2008, the Arabian stallion Destiny's Avenger, aka Avenger, the first horse I ever fell in love with, was released from his physical body and this earthly realm to rejoin great horse spirits on the other side. I grieved his loss; for in the twenty years I had known him, he had been the inspiration for thirteen works of art I created to celebrate his beauty and spirit. His famous portrait, *Avenger*, had touched countless people.

In 1988, I was twenty-one and beginning my career as an equine artist. I met Avenger when I was commissioned to paint his portrait. Avenger was a three-year-old dark bay Arabian stallion in all his glory, and I was humbled by his magnificence. As I photographed him for his portrait, Avenger awakened something in me. Time seemed suspended as I watched this graceful and majestic stallion dance a solo ballet to his own music and for me alone. My camera could not capture his presence in its entirety, but my heart did. His essence, new yet somehow familiar, infused me as surely as if he had stepped into my soul and taken up residence.

At the end of our photo session, Avenger galloped straight toward me. Although we were separated only by a tiny, decorative chain fence, I felt unafraid as he skidded to a stop and placed his head over my shoulder in a moment of grace. I put my hand to his cheek and knew I had been blessed. Through him I began to understand that the horses I had encountered in my dreams were also of this Earth.

In order to paint him accurately and do justice to his spirit, I realized I had to somehow become him. Experiencing his presence had touched me so profoundly that, amazingly, I was able to achieve this. The portrait I created of Avenger was unlike anything I had painted before and surpassed my ability. He was the first horse I had painted from life. Previously, I had worked from my imagination or from photographs, attempting to portray the image of an unknown horse with my own interpretation of the horse's power. With Avenger I didn't have to imagine. I had seen his majesty. That experience allowed me to put the feelings he had inspired into his painting.

People who saw the painting in my portfolio, in my advertising, or on greeting cards I had published remarked on its power; yet they noticed kindness in the horse's eyes. Many people also recognized their own beloved horses in Avenger's image. I came to realize that his spirit is in all horses. Now his spirit was in me. He had touched my heart and imagination in a way that influenced all my work from then on.

Avenger's owners were thrilled with the portrait and said that I had truly been able to portray his presence. This experience taught me how a work of art that is infused with love can profoundly affect those who see it.

Avenger's Journey of Destiny

When I first met Avenger he was kept at an elegant boarding stable. He had won an award as Reserve Champion halter stallion at an Arabian horse show in Scottsdale, Arizona. But his owners discovered he was being abused by the trainer, so they discontinued showing him and vowed to never again let him out of their care.

The owners began promoting him as a breeding stallion and cared for him with respect. He seemed to be leading a happy life and was exercised daily at liberty in the arena.

Over the years, whenever I was in Phoenix, I would track down Avenger's owners, who moved frequently. Sometimes the owners would board Avenger at stables; other times he would be kept at home with their horses. Each time, I noticed their financial circumstances and the horse's accommodations worsening. Yet the owners continued to express their pride, love, and commitment to Avenger, so my concerns were assuaged.

In July 1998, my letter to Avenger's owners came back with the stamp, "Forwarding Address Expired" and a new address in Oklahoma. I despaired that I had lost touch with Avenger, but I sent another letter to the new address and pleaded that his owners get in touch with me. They responded and reported that they were happily settled, and Avenger was enjoying the green pastures. Relieved that I could still visit him, I vowed to travel to see him soon. I had a feeling that all was not as it seemed.

In January 1999, I received a phone call from a woman named Chandra Faulk in Muskogee, Oklahoma. She said, "I have a greeting card from years ago of your painting of a stallion named Destiny's Avenger."

I said, "Yes, that's my artwork." I expected her to request a brochure. Instead she said, "Well, you probably aren't going to believe me, but I have the horse you painted."

A jolt went through me as I asked, "What do you mean? His owners were very devoted, and they'd never agree to sell him."

"That's what I thought," she said, "but they didn't sell him. They abandoned him and three other horses at my boarding stable here in Oklahoma."

Chandra told me how she had acquired the greeting card featuring his portrait. As a teenager ten years before, she had bought the card with Avenger's portrait on it in a tack store. She had loved it so much that she framed and hung it in her room. When she grew up, later married, and started a Tennessee Walking Horse farm, she kept it as a favorite work of art.

In 1996, she had agreed to board some horses for a new client. As a nineteen-year-old dark bay Arabian stallion was led off the client's trailer, he filled the surrounding area with his presence.

Chandra's heart skipped a beat, and then she wondered why the horse looked so familiar. Then a memory surfaced — he resembled the horse on the greeting card she still had hanging on her wall. She confirmed this with the horse's owner, who said the card had been published using his commissioned portrait. Two years later, Chandra discovered to her dismay that Avenger's owners had skipped town, leaving her with unpaid board bills and abandoning their four Arabian horses.

Kim's portrait of Destiny's Avenger

As Chandra pursued the legal aspects of taking ownership of the abandoned horses, her expenses mounted and she needed to find a home for Avenger and the other horses. One day, the framed card caught her eye. My name, as the artist, was on the back of the card. I was the only person she could think of who knew anything about Avenger and could perhaps help find someone to buy him and the other Arabians.

My mind raced while Chandra spoke. Could I rescue Avenger myself? I loved him with all my heart, and it seemed like this could be a dream come true. But later, after much wishful thinking, I came to the difficult decision that I couldn't take him. I felt a strong desire to protect him and wished he could be near me. But acquiring a stallion conflicted with my lifestyle and resources, my own horse's needs, and my belief about what was right for Avenger. Then in a meditation I received the clear impression that he was not meant to be with me. Avenger was destined for the heart of another. Although not rescuing him was one of the most difficult decisions I ever had to make, I trusted that the amazing series of events that had led Chandra to call me would also lead Avenger to his true home.

That day, I told Chandra all I knew about the horse. I begged her not to take him to a sale where his chances of finding a buyer would be slim. By this time Avenger was an older Arabian stallion, untrained as a riding horse. He wouldn't have much chance of finding a home in her area of the country. I knew full well what his dire options would be if he didn't find a home. I kept praying for his well-being and for a miracle to save him.

As the months passed I kept in touch with Chandra. I learned that she had planned to take him to a sale on several occasions but each time someone would call out of the blue and show interest in him. Then the person would not follow through.

Avenger Comes Home

In July I received a call from a client named Carol Joy Buri. An avid collector of my equine art, she wanted to stop by the studio to purchase one of my new prints. Though she didn't own any horses, she loved them.

As I showed Carol my new works, I looked up her file on my computer and remembered that in 1993 she had purchased an expensive secondary market print of the sold-out edition of Avenger's portrait. This prompted me to share the story with her about Avenger's abandonment. I began to notice how intently Carol listened. When I paused, she stood up abruptly and asked,

"He is for sale?" Bright tears appeared in her eyes. "I can't believe it, Avenger's for sale!"

Carol explained that from the time she was five years old she had received very clear images of what her soul horse would look like and a knowingness about the very special personality this horse would have. She felt in her heart that someday they would find each other and be together for the rest of their lives. But as the years had passed, the reality of ever owning the horse had faded.

In 1993 Carol had seen my portrait of Avenger and instantly known him to be her dream horse. But someone else owned him. She felt heartbroken. If she could never share her life with this horse, at least she would have his portrait.

After realizing that day that she had at last found her soul mate, Carol begged me to call Chandra immediately. Following my intuition to tell her the story had resulted in the future owner of my beloved Avenger standing here in my studio. And Carol lived only an hour away from me, so my dream would come true too. Avenger would soon be home.

Avenger lived a happy life with Carol. She later rescued his son, Count Avenger, who had also been abandoned. She purchased a black Egyptian Arabian mare she named Silky. Avenger sired a daughter, Avenger's Wind Spirit, aka Breezy, with Silky. Then Carol had Avenger gelded so he could live in harmony with his family. She and her husband built a new farm and had their road named Destiny's Haven by the State of Washington.

Over time, Carol shared with me that Avenger, a very wise teacher, had taught her lessons about life. She had learned that all the possessions and things she used to think were important became insignificant next to him. Although Carol was fifty years old and admittedly set in her ways, Avenger had revealed to her new ways of thinking and better ways of living. He had shown her how to not hold on to grudges and to be quicker to forgive wrongs. He had taught her patience and to be less demanding of those around her. She became less selfish and more understanding and developed a kinder, gentler way of treating others. Despite all the odds of it ever happening, she had been united with her destined horse and had offered him the best life she knew how to give.

In November 2007, I went to visit Avenger and Carol. Avenger's health had been deteriorating, and I sensed that it would be our last meeting on this Earth. I had the impulse to show him the picture of his portrait that I had created twenty years before. He focused on the image with great interest, repeatedly looking at it with intensity beyond mere curiosity. His daughter, Breezy, looked over his shoulder and nudged him, trying for a closer look. Carol was equally amazed that Avenger was so focused on the painting. The moment was powerful and poignant as I recalled our complex connections over the years.

Tears came to my eyes when I told Avenger how much I loved him. He lifted his head and touched his warm nostril to my lips. He breathed long and softly into me. I closed my eyes and breathed back into him. I felt lost and found at the same time. All our emotions were in our breath. It was a moment that passed in a flash and lasted for an eternity.

MEDITATION

The full-circle synchronicity of Avenger's spirit breathing life into Kim's artwork reminds us that destiny infuses the lives of horses and humans. Has an animal enhanced your mission or calling in some way?

CHAPTER THREE

Teaching

*When allowed to exist in a relatively stress-free environment,
a horse's mind is literally swirling with the nuance common
in creative geniuses. Just by associating with their equine
partners, riders can tap into this stream as well.*

— LINDA KOHANOV

DIANA: THE SAGA OF A WILD HORSE

KAREN SUSSMAN, *Lantry, South Dakota*

Diana, wild horse of the Gila herd, actually began her historic quest for freedom centuries ago. She is descended from a herd of horses brought to America in the 1600s by Father Eusebio Kino, a missionary from Spain. Diana inherited her extraordinary courage and tenacity from Father Kino's horses, who survived the trip across the ocean in small sailing vessels. Their journey took months over raging waves. The horses were strapped in slings, unable to stand, and kept in dark and dank areas of the ships. At times in an area of very rough seas, known as the Horse Latitudes, many horses were thrown overboard to preserve the integrity of the ship. By the time land was sighted, the horses who had survived had lost weight due to ever-diminishing food rations. After completing their long voyage, the horses were hoisted off the ship, thrown into the water, and made to swim ashore behind rowboats.

In 1699, Father Kino's mission was located approximately ninety miles south of Gila Bend, Arizona, on the Mexican border. By the mid-1800s, there were 20,000 wild horses roaming the south to the western part of Arizona. Many were descendants of Father Kino's Spanish mission and carried the characteristics of the Spanish horses, who were known as the greatest horses in the world at that time.

As the West continued to be settled by Europeans, who had brought thousands of cattle by the mid-1800s, wild horses on the western rangelands began to lose their freedom. Ranchers viewed wild horses as competitors to cattle for lush green grasses that grew in southern Arizona. Reports from diaries of westerners, who saw the lands for the first time, commented on the abundance of knee-high grass hitting their stirrups as they rode their steeds. Soon there were bounties of as much as $2 an ear on wild horses.

Indians were losing their lands, and the cattlemen dominated the West. Many of the cowboys became "mustangers," those who developed the art of capturing wild horses and shipping them to slaughter. The methods of capture were often inhumane. If horses deviated from the trap site, they were shot. Many horses had to run so far that their hooves wore off. Once captured, wire rings were placed around their nostrils to restrict their breathing, keeping them from running away after they had recovered. Foals were often left behind to die a frightening death without their mothers.

In the 1920s, a local mustanger named Ike Hocker was ingenious in the way he captured wild horses — not by air, or truck, but on a motorcycle. His method opened a lucrative business for the mustangers. By the time Hocker quit the business in 1936, nearly all the wild horses were gone. They had been sent to California to be ground up for chicken food.

But there was one group of wild horses Ike never caught. More than likely it was because his motorcycle could not penetrate the thick salt cedar bushes on the north side of the Gila River where the herd would hide by day and graze by night. These salt cedar bushes, which grew to be twenty feet high in an open desert landscape, became the "tree of life" for the remaining wild horses.

Even after Ike Hocker gave up mustanging, generations of the Gila herd relied on the safety of these weedlike bushes. But a new predator lurked in the shadows. Local ranchers began to shoot the wild horses, whom they considered vermin. There was to be no competition from wild horses taking a blade of grass from their cattle or sharing in the alfalfa fields.

President Teddy Roosevelt, a conservationist, had brought the salt cedar bush, known as tamarisk, from the Middle East to Arizona. He had it planted all along the banks of the Gila River. Roosevelt thought that the tamarisk would help to preserve water in the river, never realizing that the plant drinks more than its share of water and then some.

Around the 1930s and 1940s the desert landscape was changing rapidly. In the harsh climate irrigated water was necessary for growing hay, and the once-navigable Gila River became a dry wash bed. Its waters were diverted to alfalfa fields planted in the hot desert soil, where temperatures rise to 120 degrees Fahrenheit and above. Today, because of the pesticides running off the alfalfa fields, the waters remain polluted and unfit for human or animal.

Enter Diana

Diana, proud descendent of the original herd, was born in the late 1970s. She was the usual size for Spanish horses, not more than 14 hands. She had all the traits of the Sorraia wild horses of Spain, an ancient base stock, primeval in character, from the Iberian Peninsula where horses were first domesticated. Dun in color, considered the color of prehistoric horses, she had a stripe down her back that served to disguise her at night, in the full moon, and keep predators away. Diana had primitive markings on her legs known as zebra striping. Her large eyes appeared to hold the wisdom of the ancients. Her demeanor was that of a goddess. Her presence made a mere mortal feel small and insignificant.

As a young filly, Diana roamed the desert areas near Gila Bend, where the last surviving Gila herd remained. The 1970s were a time when most wild horses should have been safe from harassment, capture, and threat of death. Public Law 92-195 had passed in 1971, protecting all wild horses on public lands, defined as Forest Service or Bureau of Land Management (BLM) lands. Diana and her herd lived on BLM lands. Unfortunately the herd had never been recognized as "wild and free roaming." This meant they weren't protected under the law until 1996 because of a false assumption that these horses belonged to the Native American Indians. The Gila herd would at last receive federal recog-

Karen's Diana (right) with two other wild horses

nition and protection because of the efforts of the International Society for the Protection of Mustangs and Burros (ISPMB).

Public Law 92-195 protecting wild horses had passed thanks to the efforts of the ISPMB's first president, Velma Johnston, affectionately known as Wild Horse Annie. Annie was extraordinary, a woman who was years before her time. Although disfigured from polio at a time in American culture when most women were not outspoken public figures, Annie campaigned for twenty years on behalf of America's wild horses. She became an inspiration, especially to women, as one person changing the world. She brought awareness to the American people that government public lands were for everyone and not for special interests.

Before Annie died in 1977, she had adopted a wild horse; I decided to follow in her footsteps. Since 1976, I'd had an application into the BLM to adopt a wild horse, even though most trainers told me not to adopt a wild horse because I would get killed. I'd been warned that wild horses are inbred, stupid, and dangerous. It was this lack of understanding of wild horses among the horse industry that led me to champion their cause. In 1981, I adopted a nine-month-old wild horse, Shooting Star. If anything, Shooting Star was more trustworthy, expressive, full of life, and intelligent than any horse I had ever known. Star and I remained partners for life. I truly felt that she came from the heavens — hence, her name. Shooting Star died at the young age of twenty. Every time I see a shooting star, tears well up in my eyes, because I know she is saying hello. Shooting Star inspired me to do everything possible to save Diana and the Gila herd when they most needed me.

The Gila Herd in Danger

In 1988 I became ISPMB's third president. In 1999 ISPMB received notification that the Gila horses would be removed and were considered estray, meaning domestic horses gone wild. The notification piqued my interest, since even though I lived in Arizona and had been volunteering for ISPMB since 1983, I hadn't known wild horses still existed in the central part of my state. I spent three months interviewing local ranchers and gaining an in-depth history of the horses. Ultimately I achieved the goal of saving from elimination in Arizona six wild burro herds as well as Diana and her Gila herd.

After federal protection was afforded to Diana's herd in 1996, the local ranchers knew that if they shot a wild horse they would pay a $100,000 fine. The previous fine for killing a wild horse had been $2,000. The first federal district to raise the fines was in Arizona, coming shortly after the 1990 Good Friday massacre of forty-nine wild burros in Kingman. ISPMB initiated the first meeting between the BLM and Arizona federal prosecutors. Within the following three years, all federal districts in the United States adopted the new sentencing guidelines and higher fines.

With federal protections finally in place, it appeared that Diana and her herd could live out their lives in peace and tranquility, in Gila Bend, on their 56,000-acre herd area. But this was not meant to be. In 1999, the BLM removed the entire herd, citing a technicality in Public Law 92-195. Landowners could request that the BLM remove "problem" animals grazing their private lands. Since the wild horses maintained their freedom by grazing alfalfa fields that had been planted years before, they did not understand the boundary changes that made it possible to legally turn them into trespassers on private lands. After all, there were no fences on private lands to keep out the wild horses. Ranchers didn't have to fence their lands, because cattle have the right to graze anywhere in the West, on your land or my land.

As far back as 1996, the BLM had wanted to remove the horses, so it was an easy decision for the agency to legally eliminate them in 1999. The BLM removed thirty-six animals from the lands where they had lived since the 1600s. In 2000, ISPMB negotiated with the BLM to adopt Diana and the rare Gila herd and bring them to our conservation program on the Pine Ridge Indian Reservation in South Dakota. Four horses were killed in the BLM roundup. One of the four was euthanized by the BLM. The horse had survived on three legs with a broken front leg and a bullet hole in his neck. No doubt, the horse had fallen after being shot, breaking his leg. The wild horse had survived these injuries only to meet his final fate at the hands of the BLM cowboys. Another individual adopted one stallion from the roundup. This left thirty-one wild horses, who would soon be under the care of ISPMB.

The Gila herd was the second wild-horse herd to be rescued by the ISPMB. Maintaining wild herds in a conservation program takes an enormous amount of funding and constant observation. But the handwriting on the wall prompted ISPMB to begin taking in endangered and rare herds. In 1971, there were 303 wild herd areas designated in ten western states. In 2009, there are only 199 herds left. More herds faced elimination with the continuous pressure from cattlemen in the ever-growing demand for dwindling grasses.

The Gila herd were transported to Phoenix and remained in holding pens until May 2000, when the harsh South Dakota winter would subside. Even before the herd's arrival in South Dakota, one of ISPMB's volunteers named its lead mare Diana, after the Roman goddess. Living up to her name and heritage, Diana showed that she was the protector of her herd. She would signal alerts by snorting and turning to run when dangerous humans appeared. To Diana, anything that walked on two legs could not be trusted.

Diana was beginning to feel comfortable in Phoenix after several months went by. We noted that she wouldn't snort when we entered the pen, although she never took her eyes off us. Then one day, trucks came to pick up the herd for the long drive to South Dakota. The horses had to be pushed into a loading area and up a ramp to the large semi truck. This was no small task in an area not designed for loading horses. The little trust in humans that Diana was beginning to show quickly evaporated.

On a memorable warm June day, Diana was turned loose to be wild and free at the ISPMB-leased lands in South Dakota. As the horses left their corrals, Diana took the lead at a full gallop. She raced across the entire five hundred acres to a tree line on the property that stood several thousand feet above the drop-off into the Badlands. She was heading to safety and taking her herd with her.

After letting the herd rest for several hours, we climbed in our four-wheel truck to move them to the open land and push them slowly to their watering site. After they knew where the water was, we could rest assured that they would explore every aspect of that pasture from every direction.

From the first day of her arrival, Diana kept her distance from people. Horses have excellent memories, and she had experienced how untrustworthy humans could be. But Diana was a survivor. She and her herd lived through their first harsh winter in South Dakota. Although ISPMB had paid more than twice the normal fee for the lease of the pasture near the Badlands, there was not enough forage. The rancher who owned the pasture had decided to put his cattle out with the wild horses. Diana nearly starved and had to be brought into the main ranch with another stallion and put on extra feed.

This was the turning point for Diana and her herd. As ISPMB's president, I bought a beautiful ranch just four hours north of the Badlands on the Cheyenne River Sioux Reservation. We moved all the horses from the Badlands ranch and brought them safely to their new home in Lantry, South Dakota, in December 2001.

Diana would now be free to live out her life in a place where she would never have to worry. By then, her face had turned completely gray. The fearful glint that shone in her beautiful brown eyes when she looked at people diminished with each passing year.

Diana and the Gila Horse Teachers

In the safety of our ranch in Lantry, we were able to observe the Gila herd doing what came naturally. The horses banded up in harems. The young bachelors had their own band, and the dominant, majestic stallions sorted out their mares. Diana was the oldest horse in the entire herd. Her stallion's name was Ian, the youngest harem stallion. Ian treated Diana with the greatest respect and protected her from the younger bachelor stallions.

Diana never foaled after she was captured, but there is no doubt that many of her offspring were already part of the herd. Blood typing and genetic testing had been done when the herd was first captured. According to the geneticist, all the Gila horses were Spanish and closely related to one another. There was no outside blood from other breeds. In fact, Diana's herd presented one of the most stable herds, because the harems had not been disrupted in more than fifty years.

The Gila herd presented a marked contrast to what was being done to wild horses from 1990 to the present. Most herds managed by the BLM are removed every three years or more to keep down their numbers. Although the BLM allows older horses and mares to go back to their lands, once the harems have been disrupted, they never band up the same way again. Usually younger stallions steal the mares, a trend that is gradually destroying the wonderful educational system that has been in place for the past five hundred years. Older and wiser stallions are the strongest force in maintaining harmony in the herds. However, when the harems are disturbed, the younger and stronger animals have a greater opportunity to take charge. It's analogous to having fifth graders running a neighborhood. Without having access to the older stallions' wisdom, the younger horses are not competent to teach new generations. With such disorganization of band structures, the stallions start breeding fillies when the fillies are only one year old instead of four. As a result, fertility rates among wild horse herds have skyrocketed from 10 percent to more than 20 percent under BLM management practices. The increasing fertility rate of the herds is the direct result of harem bands being destroyed as stallions are separated from their mares when captured.

The dismantling of wild-horse family units has occurred because of human ignorance; many people do not understand these incredible creatures as they are in the wild. Just as wolves look like dogs but are different, so it is with wild and domestic horses. Wild horses cannot and should not be managed in the same way as domestic livestock. Because we have kept Diana's herd intact in conditions that are natural to wild horses, the herd has been able to teach us the importance of keeping harems together and of allowing the wild horses to maintain strong social bonds. ISPMB's receiving of the Gila herd with little or no intervention in all its years in the wild was nothing short of a miracle. For ten years the Gila herd has been the perfect study for natural wild-horse behaviors, unaltered by humankind. ISPMB has been able to create a model management program showing a contrast to the devastating effects of repeated wild horse removals from public lands.

A scientist proved me right about one of the aspects of wild horses that those of us who understand these animals inside and out already know in our hearts to be true. In 1990, the nation's leading equine geneticist, Ernest (Gus) G. Cothran Jr., PhD, at Texas A & M University, said that wild horses have more genetic diversity than any breed of domestic horse. Wild horses are not inbred. I believe that wild horses are the greatest horses alive. But I wondered if Diana would ever grow to appreciate us humans as we at ISPMB appreciate her kind.

At our ranch on the South Dakota plains, Diana once again had trees and plenty of hiding places with water and abundant forage. She was free in a way that all animals should be — as the law states, "Free from harassment, capture, and death." Diana was free to be with Ian and her family — never to be separated. Free as the wind.

In 2004, tours began to visit this rare Gila herd. I noticed a remarkable change in Diana. She would come up to the truck to investigate the visitors who had arrived. She no longer snorted, stamped her feet, or ran to the nearest tree.

To everyone's amazement, after all she had suffered at the hands of humans, including being chased and shot at, Diana had forgiven humankind for its intolerance and greed. Visitors and supporters who learned about Diana and the Gila herd honored this courageous lead mare. Diana and her herd had demonstrated that all life is interrelated and must be held in reverence, a lesson yet to be learned by humanity.

One day in July 2005, Diana was not with her band to greet us. This beautiful summer day Diana had passed peacefully into the spirit world, leaving behind those of us who loved her dearly. We will forever carry her lessons of honoring, understanding, and respecting all living creatures in our hearts and share them with the world. We hope someday soon to have enough acreage for all of our four herds to run wild and free as the Gilas do. We hope that our dreams will be realized in bringing our conservation model to many areas of our country and to develop ecotourism nationally and worldwide. May Diana's legacy be that we preserve the heritage of America, the remaining wild horse herds.

MEDITATION

By protecting her herd, Diana taught Karen and others the ways of wild horses. How have you uplifted and enlightened many people by saving or helping one animal?

ROCKY, THE RESCUED HORSE WHO IS CHANGING A COMMUNITY

❖

ANNETTE FISHER, *Ravenna, Ohio*

M y husband, Russ, and I moved in 1998 to Ravenna Township, about a twenty-minute drive east of Akron, Ohio. We were attracted to this mostly flat land with peaceful woods that contain hundreds of trees, but we did not come here with the intention of starting a sanctuary. Our initial dream was to live in this country setting and have one horse. Now, 385 horses later, the non-profit organization my husband and I started, Happy Trails Farm Animal Sanctuary, Inc., is an all-volunteer labor of love. Normally we have between 100 and 150 animals on the farm. Every one of them comes from an abuse or neglect situation. Nearly every type of farm animal is represented: ducks, geese, chickens, turkeys, sheep, goats, pot-bellied pigs, and horses. Smaller shelters for pigs, chickens, and ducks dot these ten acres, while the horses live in a big, two-story barn with fourteen stalls.

Working with only private donations and fundraisers, Happy Trails Farm Animal Sanctuary helps with mass rescues, such as breaking up a cock-fighting ring, and many farm rescues for the state of Ohio. We support the local humane and animal protection officers when they get requests to investigate farm animal abuse, and we are often called in to assist with court cases. When our farm fills up, we use foster homes for the overflow animals. Because of its relatively small size, ours is not a place where animals come to retire, but we rehabilitate and then move them to permanent homes. One horse, Rocky, became a beacon of hope for positive changes within a community and an emblem of the joy that rescued farm animals can bring to loving families.

The Amish Horse Dilemma

Rocky started his life as an Amish horse. Our farm is located between two of the largest Amish communities in Ohio. In their hilly area of the state, the Amish use horses for transportation and fieldwork. People see pictures of Amish horse-drawn carriages, but the underside of this idyllic image is what happens to the animals after they are too old or infirm to be of use. More than 90 percent of the Amish horses go to auctions when they can no longer serve as buggy or plow horses.

In 2008, horse slaughter was outlawed in the United States. This fact misleads the general public into believing that horses are no longer sold to meat buyers. The 2008 U.S. law only keeps horses from being slaughtered in the United States. But meat buyers purchase horses and ship them under terrible conditions to Mexico or Canada. In Mexico, horse slaughter is unregulated and absolutely horrific.

In May 2008, our organization did an awareness campaign about the Sugar Creek Auction, the second largest horse auction east of the Mississippi. We purchased twenty-five draft horses who were for sale and raised more than $30,000 to pay for their medical care and find new adoptive families for them. At that time, every Friday at the Sugar Creek Auction, two hundred to three hundred horses were being sold to meat buyers. The owner of Sugar Creek has been severely fined by the U.S. Department of

Agriculture (USDA) for violations of animal safety regulations in transporting horses.

In an effort to intercede in the fates of Amish horses, we started the Amish Horse Retirement Program. It is designed to assist Amish families who have a horse who can no longer pull a buggy or plow for medical reasons or old age. The acceptance criteria for the program are that the Amish owner directly surrenders and donates the horse. These horses then are given an overall health and wellness medical examination, are updated with vaccinations and a consistent worming schedule, have their hooves trimmed, and are made available for adoption.

Annette's Rocky

Usually the horses have worked hard most of their lives, plowing fields and pulling buggies. We try to make them as comfortable as possible and find adoptive homes where they will retire to be loved and spoiled for the rest of their lives. We keep the Amish families in touch with their horse's new adoptive families, so they can see how the animals are being taken care of and assured that the horse was not sent to slaughter.

Some Amish horses we get have been used far past their prime. Most Amish horses are not wormed or vaccinated. Their hooves may have not been trimmed or reshod in quite some time. But the people love their horses enough to choose the alternative of our retirement program to selling them at auction.

Because we believe that it is important for Amish horse owners to be better educated about their horses' needs, in 2006 we started the Amish Horse Health Seminars to teach horse health care to the Amish community. At one of the educational seminars we held, where a veterinarian provided instruction, more than fifty Amish folks attended. At the seminars, we give out enough horse wormer for the attendees' entire farms. We offer transportation to and from the seminar and refreshments while people are there. In addition, we pass out blankets to the Amish community every winter for their horses.

As a result of all these efforts, Happy Trails Farm Animal Sanctuary has made friends with many Amish community members. Because we go into each situation trying not to judge a lifestyle or culture, we get repeat calls from families who are about to retire their horses. They know that our only objective is to help the animals. All this care in building positive relationships with the Amish paid off when Rocky needed our help.

Rocky's Rescue

In 2003 we received an unusual call from an Amish family about a Percheron horse who was not one of those who were too old to work. Instead, this horse turned out to be a ten-month-old baby named Rocky. Apparently the family's home on a hillside didn't have much, if any, pasture space available for daily exercise of their horses. Consequently, the foal had spent his entire life inside an eight-by-eight-foot stall with no exercise. Rocky had moved around and gotten his halter stuck on some broken boards located high on the stall wall. The family had found him hanging by his neck. They managed to free the horse, but the accident caused facial paralysis, so Rocky had problems eating afterward. Weak from malnutrition, he was of no use to the family. Fortunately, they didn't want to send him through the auctions.

We asked one of our volunteers to pick up Rocky and take him to our facility. A pathetic creature, Rocky arrived in very bad shape. His legs were caked with manure and bowed C-shape because his tendons were severely contracted. Rocky's hair was filled with lice. Our veterinarian examined the horse, and his prognosis was not good. He believed that Rocky was beyond rehabilitation. His back legs had suffered so badly from atrophy that he would never be able to walk normally or hold his weight as he grew up.

We don't often second-guess the vet, but there was something about this horse that made us say we would like to give him a chance. If he wasn't suffering, we wanted to work with Rocky for several weeks. Reluctantly the vet agreed to our plan but advised us to keep in touch and report back about the horse's progress. I wanted to provide Rocky with every opportunity and use every avenue to help him recover and have good chance at life.

Rocky stayed at his foster home for several months. He gained weight. His legs straightened out. His muscle mass and tone increased. We brought him back to Happy Trails and continued to work with him. We treated his face where the halter had dug in. We walked him continually to strengthen his legs.

One of our volunteers, Dick Zampini, a retired Happy Trails volunteer and former horse owner, enjoyed working with Rocky. Dick groomed, cared for, and fed Rocky, helping him to heal. After several months of care, Rocky filled out his legs and was able to have fun playing with the other horses. By 2004 he had a growth spurt. In spite of his early trauma, Rocky grew into a large horse who now stands at 18.1 hands and weighs between 1,800 and 2,000 pounds.

We wanted to expose Rocky to more people. He was a sterling example of success with our Amish Horse Retirement Program and perhaps could win more support for it. Dick decided to show Rocky in the halter class at the Portage County Fair in the two-year-old class. Rocky was still a stallion. Because of his prior malnutrition and need for growth and recovery, we had not been able to geld him. By the time we made the decision to train Rocky for competing in the fair as a stallion, we had only two weeks left to prepare him.

In the summer of 2004 I called Ken Aberegg, a horse trainer who has experience with draft horses. We wanted Ken to help Dick get Rocky ready for his public debut. Sarah Richards, another of our volunteers, also helped with the training by trotting behind Rocky and waving a small lunge whip in the air to encourage forward motion.

Dick says, "Rocky seemed to be a natural. He would trot when asked and stop on command with all four feet exactly where they were supposed to be. Our relationship deepened as we worked together. Rocky has a very nice disposition and is always a gentleman who never kicked or stepped on anybody. He's fond of peppermint candy and liked it that Sarah always carried the treat with her. Any time he heard a candy wrap crinkle, he knew it meant something good for him." At that time, Rocky was still too small to be ridden, but he enjoyed running and playing with horses in the field. He liked to take the occasional gentle nip at another horse's backside in a playful way. He loved being a horse and doing what horses do. Yet Rocky grew to totally trust Dick and to the best of his ability would do whatever Dick asked.

At last, it was time for Dick to show Rocky to the Portage County Fair. Every morning at the fair Dick would take Rocky for an exercise walk. One day, in an uncharacteristic move, Rocky refused to cross a four-inch-wide tar patch on the road. He planted his feet firmly on the ground and wouldn't budge. Dick decided to try something he'd done with another horse. He turned Rocky around and had him back up over the tar patch. It worked. They went to the exercise area where Rocky walked, trotted, stretched out, and nibbled on some pasture grass.

Later, when Dick showed Rocky in front of the judges, the horse did exactly as he had done with the tar patch. He planted his feet perfectly on the ground, except this time, it was something he was supposed to do for the competition. The other competitors wondered how Dick had gotten the horse to perform so well.

Even though he'd had only two weeks of training, Rocky won first place for his age group of stallions and also won reserve grand champion, which is like a best-in-show competition of all the Percherons. After receiving the award Dick tucked the first-place blue ribbon inside his belt. When he bent over to check Rocky's feet to make sure they were square, Rocky plucked the ribbon from Dick's belt, held it in his mouth, and nibbled on it. The crowd laughed and enjoyed the moment. After all, it was Rocky's ribbon.

Rocky Finds a Forever Home

After Rocky won at the county fair we brought him back to the sanctuary. A few months later, Eileen and Bob Roloff, a very nice couple, came to us looking for a draft horse. They were thinking of getting a young horse to work with and train so he would grow up and become part of their family.

Eileen and Bob met and fell in love with Rocky. They knew Rocky would require a lot of work and training. The veterinarian thought that when Rocky got older, he could be ridden and do light cart work. The Roloffs decided to adopt Rocky.

To prepare Rocky to go to his new home, we again sent him to Ken Aberegg's training facility in Alliance, Ohio; Rocky spent several months with him. Ken taught Rocky how to be ridden and saddled. He was harnessed and began learning how to ground drive in preparation for pulling a cart. Ground-drive training consists of the trainer walking behind the horse, holding on to incredibly long reins, and then telling the horse to go forward. And Rocky grew and grew. By the time he returned to us and then went to live with the Roloff family, he had become a big, solid black horse who towered over everything in the barn.

Eileen tells us that Rocky has turned into their gentle giant. He squeezes himself into the hay room to filch bites of hay. To get him out of there, they softly say, "Ba-ah-ah-ack." They find it to be quite an accomplishment and humbling to move a ton of horse with only a softly spoken word.

Rocky is also the barn comedian. Eileen says, "Rocky gently turns the lights on and off in the barn if he thinks I haven't done that job soon enough. He stands sideways in front of the fan in the summer so the cool breeze blows over his whole body. He loves to drink warm water and eat pieces of peppermint candy cane. He is best friends with Eagle, another of our horses. And he's learning to drive a cart."

Eileen tells about a blustery winter day in January 2009. She made her usual late night rounds to the barn in a snowstorm. She tucked in Rocky and her Appaloosa, Eagle, for the night by giving them hay, water, and a treat. She says that as she walked back to her house she thought about how lucky Rocky and Eagle are and wondered how many other horses had nothing to eat and no shelter or were locked in a stall from which they could never escape. She said, "I think Rocky's mission is to be a constant reminder that there are many more Rockys out there, and we can't forget them. Rocky is our treasure."

Rocky's success has inspired us to tell more people about and support our Amish Horse Retirement Program and the other animals at Happy Trails Farm Animal Sanctuary. A couple of years after Rocky left the farm, we started letting people sponsor an animal. Sponsors receive their animals' pictures and life stories. We invite them to come to the farm and visit the animals they sponsor. A lot of people in Ohio drive here over the holidays and spend the day with their sponsored pigs, geese, and horses.

Rocky and every horse we rescue inspires us. I had a Native American friend who gave me a medicine bag because he said we're like the medicine men of old. I save a piece of mane or tail from each of our rescued horses who has passed on and place it in the medicine bag. This means that we have taken the lessons from that horse onward to help the next ones. Maybe from a horse we learned how to treat a medical issue or how to be a better person. I keep adding to the medicine bag and remember its accumulation of life lessons.

From Rocky I have learned that sometimes people give up before they even try. We often get animals people have judged as being hopeless. Rocky taught me to follow the beliefs that are deep in my heart even when not everyone agrees with me. I learned that getting good things to happen takes perseverance, a strong faith, and trust in my gut instinct that things will work out in a good way.

MEDITATION

Rocky has become the poster horse for re-homing Amish horses and opened doors for Annette to assist the entire community. Has a horse or other animal you have known served through teaching by example?

PIPER LED ME INTO
THE WORLD OF HORSES

LAURA REDGRAVE, *Los Angeles, California*

Have you ever been introduced into a world that you never imagined you would enter? That's what happened to me. My very good friend Galen, who owned a horse named Odin, wanted me to come out to the stable and see her world and what it is like to be with horses. She had spoken about this different kind of lifestyle, and I must admit, I was curious.

Galen's stable was a place where a person could get dirty and dusty and not care how she looked. I enjoyed myself, except for one huge dilemma — I appeared to be allergic to horses. My eyes itched and my neck broke into rashes when I was around horses. I thought, "Just as well. Horses are an expensive hobby. I'm much better off without them."

A few months had passed when Galen came to me, looking excited and giddy about a filly her good friend Mary wanted to sell. I reminded Galen of what had occurred at my last meeting with a horse. "I'm allergic," I said. "There's no way!" I had never owned a horse, so why and how would I purchase a filly now? Experts recommend that an inexperienced rider should not purchase a young horse; it's a recipe for disaster. I was most definitely not looking for a horse. In spite of all those logical reasons not to, Galen talked me into meeting Piper.

As I walked past all the horses in their large pens with pipe fencing, I was thinking, "This filly can't be that pretty." I was wrong. She was, indeed, beautiful. Standing at about 14 hands, Piper was a light, cream-colored buckskin with a black tail and mane, big, sweet, brown eyes, and smoky-colored lips that begged to be squished, like a baby's cheek.

I stood at Piper's stall, looking at her, smelling her, and imagining what it would be like to own such a majestic and dynamic creature. I envisioned myself feeding her carrots, brushing her mane, and riding her with the wind in my hair. I felt captivated and moved. Oddly enough, I did not have an allergic reaction this time. I decided to give myself a sixty-day trial period to see if Piper and I were a match.

After our introduction I went to the stable every day and groomed Piper. Galen would pony her out with Odin, and off they would go. Other days, Galen assisted me in the ring. Totally intimidated by Piper's size and power, I moved very slowly and cautiously. Galen used a lunge line, which is a fifteen- to thirty-foot-long rope. She would hold one end, with the other end attached to Piper's bridle. Galen wanted to train me in an English saddle. Piper had played polo in her younger years and was familiar with that discipline. I believed if I could stay seated in that saddle, riding in a western saddle would be like sitting on a couch.

Riding atop Piper was such an awesome feeling. It was a different experience for me to saddle a live animal who can do anything at any time. We went around and around the ring at a snail's pace, which for me was all I needed and wanted. Piper never took on my nervousness. Instead, she stayed very calm, perhaps almost bored. Galen always encouraged me by saying, "Good job, Laura." They were both patient and understanding, which made me want to be around Piper and learn more.

I felt a strong need to connect with Piper and looked forward to waking up every morning and seeing her. Even while driving through traffic to get to the barn, I had a smile on my face, anticipating the time I would spend with her.

One afternoon, while I was contemplating purchasing Piper, my telephone rang. It was one of my best friends, who lives five hundred miles away. In itself that is a normal occurrence, but when my friend's name appeared for the first time on my new caller ID, it read, "PIPER, D." Later that day, I started my shift as a server in a local restaurant by offering two ladies cocktails. "We'd like a bottle of Piper Sonoma Champagne," they responded. The signs were there. I needed to buy this horse.

Would Piper Be Mine?

While I was becoming attached to Piper, Galen told me that Mary had found a buyer for her. She said, "Don't worry about that." Galen was always positive and professed to know the outcome of such undecided events. I put all my faith in Galen's words and continued to go out to the stable. Soon it was time for my first trail ride, guided by Galen via the reins. To my surprise, Mary was also along for the ride on Piper's mother, Girl. It was a clear, warm day, and we were riding in Griffith Park, which is part of the Santa Monica Mountains. Throughout the entire ride, no one mentioned a word about my interest in Piper.

We returned to the stable, and Mary left. That's when Galen broke the disturbing news. Piper's prospective buyer had come out that morning to meet with Mary and Piper's veterinarian to have her evaluated before purchase. Apparently the vet could not say enough good things about Piper's conformation. By all accounts she was an amazing horse. Mary had set an asking price of $10,000, and the prospective owner had offered $8,000 cash.

When Galen told me this, my heart sank and my eyes filled

with tears. I had spent two months caring for an animal I would watch going to a man who had never spent one day with her. But I had no choice. I could not compete with that kind of money.

In a last-ditch effort to purchase Piper, I decided to plead my case with Mary. I've always believed that you never have anything to lose by trying, only regrets if you don't. I would never have forgiven myself if I let Piper go without at least expressing my feelings to Mary.

I drove home from the stable, composed myself, and made the call. I said to Mary, "I just wanted you to know, that for the last two months I have been going out every day and spending hours with Piper. Today was our very first trail ride together, and I absolutely adore her. I know that you made a deal with someone, but I had to tell you how I felt."

Laura's Piper

I was relieved to have conveyed my feelings, although I didn't expect it to make a difference in Mary's decision. "I can't believe it was your first time on her," she said. "You look like you've been riding for years. And I had no idea you have been going out there all this time. I watched you and could see your love for her."

What Mary said next took me by surprise. "I really don't want Piper to be taken away somewhere else. I'd like to keep her in the area. I would love for you to have her." Her words sunk in, but they made little difference. I told Mary how much I appreciated the offer, and it meant a lot to me, but I wasn't bargaining. I did not have the kind of money to buy Piper.

"How's $3,000?" she asked. "And you can pay it to me when you can. We'll work something out."

I was overwhelmed. My heart was so full of love for Mary at that moment that I couldn't speak. Mary had selected me to have Piper. She might have been concerned with what the other potential owner would do with her, whether it be breeding or selling. She wanted Piper to be loved by one person for her whole life and believed I was that person. Mary understood how I felt about a horse she loved. She knew Piper and I were meant to be together.

Learning about Horse-World from Piper

Piper and I both went down a path we had never traveled. I never had a horse; she never had one person to care for only her. I knew nothing about horses, and we grew together into the kind of relationship that is romanticized in novels. We respect and listen to each other. I understand the connection between a human and a horse now. I continue to feel the same vibration as that first night I met her. I understand her need to be free, to be in a herd, and to live her life as a horse. She knows I am her human, and that I make it possible for her to fulfill those needs.

I had peeked into the future by seeing Girl, Piper's mom, and knew Piper would develop ever so nicely. Just as expected, Piper has a great disposition. Of course, she can be stubborn when she chooses, but she is also curious and intelligent.

She makes me laugh. I play kickball with her, and she draws a crowd. When we are riding with the geldings, she is quick to alert them as to who is the boss. She pins her ears way back and gives them a quick snap of the head. We all laugh, because Piper knows who she is. I always say, "Oh Pie, that face, only a mother could love."

We have a manmade lake in the middle of the pasture where Piper stays. During the summer, when it's not too full, Piper makes a beeline every day for the swimming hole. She walks in, lies down, and rolls around in the water. When she emerges, more than half her body is covered in mud, and she couldn't be happier. Of the twenty-seven horses living in the pasture, Piper is the only one who appreciates a good spa day.

When Piper was boarded in pipe stalls at the ranch, before she was placed in the pasture, she had a neighbor horse who lived a couple of stalls from her. His name is Amecito. He rolls his head in circles, I believe, purely out of boredom. I tell Piper, "Do Amecito head circles," and she does them on cue.

Piper especially loves little children. She definitely understands that they are small and fragile. She allows them to place their hands under her nose and is very gentle. One day, while I held Piper with a lead rope, a mom placed her little girl, who was about three years old and suffered from a physical disability, on Piper's back. While the mother held on to her child, Piper simply stood still, and her young rider smiled with joy.

Piper has been in my life since October 2002. She lives in a huge pasture at a private, 1,000-acre ranch in Malibu among many horses, including her boyfriend, Gibson, and her best friend, Bambi, as well as an assortment of domestic and exotic animals. She is not in the least disturbed by their quacks, moos, hee-haws, shapes, stripes, bumps, or lumps. She rides through vineyards and avocado trees and looks out over mountains and sunsets. I love her beyond words and will care for her always.

Piper introduced me to a lifestyle that is pristine and natural, and to firsthand experiences of how incredibly patient, giving, and appreciative horses can be. I escape every day to a sanctuary of tranquility with her where the air is clean, my mind is clear, and I live in the moment. Merely sitting on a rock and watching the herds communicate, play, and protect one another is a sight to behold. With my friends every weekend, I ride through the vineyards, park, and mountains that overlook the ocean.

I truly thank Galen for the path, Mary for the blessing, and

Piper for introducing me to the world of horses — a fulfilling place of sheer, childlike happiness and unconditional love.

MEDITATION

Have you ever wondered, like Laura did, what is so fascinating about the world of horses? Could you allow Piper or another horse to introduce you to its secret charms?

FINDING BALANCE WITH BLONDIE

KAREN KUKLA SPIES, *Castro Valley, California*

I met Blondie on a hot September day in 2007. She was standing in a quiet pasture at a gated horse training facility in Petaluma, California, with a broodmare and several other babies. Blondie was a beautiful palomino. Her body was as bronze as a Hawaiian Tropic model's, and her mane and tail were a California beach-baby blonde. Blondie was sweet, cuddly even, and she willingly followed me around. Her eyes were soft, her disposition gentle. She looked at me intelligently. She smelled every inch of me as though she were assessing me. "Is it possible to connect to a horse so thoroughly in one short meeting?" I wondered. Maybe.

I was meeting Blondie in person that September day because of a conspiracy that had occurred a few months earlier at the Anthony Chabot Equestrian Center in the Oakland hills where my twelve-year-old daughter, Katie, and I had been taking riding lessons and working with the horses for two years. My friends Michelle and Frank, who were Blondie's owners, and my riding instructor, Vijoa, have been friends for years, with their horses boarded in the same barn only a few stalls apart at Chabot. Michelle and Vijoa had placed a picture of Blondie in Vijoa's foot-locker, which was in the tack-up area of the stable, where I would be sure to see it. Each week as part of my lesson, I groomed and tacked up one of Vijoa's horses. The saddles were kept in the tack room, and the bridles in Vijoa's footlocker. When I went to retrieve a bridle and saw Blondie's picture, I had to know everything about this horse, just as they had hoped.

Michelle and Vijoa's setup for me to find the photo fulfilled

Karen's Blondie

their prediction that I'd fall in love at first sight with Blondie. They thought Blondie and I would make a good match. Blondie was young and still growing, so she needed a fairly small rider. Since I am five-feet, five-inches tall and of medium build, Michelle thought I would be just the right size for riding Blondie. Vijoa knew that I wanted to ride more often. She thought I could do so with Blondie. Plus, I had told Frank that I'd always dreamed of

owning a Tennessee Walker one day, and Blondie was a Tennessee Walker.

"Who is this gorgeous creature?" I asked Vijoa while I looked at the photo. She told me that Michelle and Frank were looking for someone to sponsor Blondie. They wanted to move Blondie from Petaluma to Chabot, where they boarded their other two animals, a Tennessee Walking Horse named Couch and a gaited mule named Pipi who could move like a Tennessee Walker by trotting with the front legs while walking with the back legs. Frank and Michelle were hoping to find a sponsor for Blondie who would pay part of her board in exchange for riding privileges. I had never sponsored a horse before, but it was the logical next step for me, since I wasn't ready to own a horse yet but wanted to ride more often than my weekly lesson. My daughter, Katie, liked riding; I loved it.

My History with Horses

Although I was nearing fifty when I began riding at Chabot, my love affair with horses started when I was seven years old. Every year of my childhood, our family joined four other families for a weeklong summer vacation at Silver Lake in Wisconsin. All the kids would go horseback riding as often as money allowed. We even gave up swimming and water-skiing to be with horses. After four or five years, we asked our parents to just drop us off at the ranch in the morning and pick us up in time for dinner.

We were barn rats. We hung out all day and did odd jobs while continually waiting for an opportunity to ride. We toted hay and scooped poop. If we were lucky, we got to brush, lead, hold, or otherwise directly interact with the horses. The payoff was usually a free trail ride that involved crossing a shallow stream and moving at a canter or gallop. We were only beginner riders. I remember thinking, "I don't want to fall off at this speed." Yet in spite of needing to hold on for dear life, riding horses was thrilling.

The childhood love of horses cemented during my teenage years. At fourteen, I took my first horseback riding lessons. My mom drove me an hour each way to an equestrian center. I rode in an English saddle for the first time and began dressage lessons. I loved learning how subtle cues by the rider resulted in specific behaviors on a well-trained dressage horse.

A year later, I was offered a Tennessee Walking Horse for free. He gave me the smoothest ride I had ever experienced. I learned that Tennessee Walkers have a very smooth gait that other horses do not. The lesson horses I had been riding would trot, which can be very bouncy for the rider. To minimize the bumpiness, we were taught how to post the trot, which is to rise up out of the saddle every other step the horse takes. But the Tennessee Walker's special gait required no posting. It felt like I was riding on air.

I wanted that horse. But at age fifteen, I was neither employed nor driving, so I had to decline the offer. I understood the practicality of the situation, but it broke my heart. From that moment on, I swore if I could ever own a horse, it would be a Tennessee Walker. I wanted to enjoy that smooth ride again. I filed the memory away along with the hope that someday my wish would come true.

Blondie and I Begin Our Journey

Thirty-five years later, enter Miss Blonde Ambition, aka Blondie, the Tennessee Walker I had always hoped to have. Even though I wouldn't own her, I would be her sole sponsor and rider.

This could be viewed as a story about how a young girl's horse dream came true later in life. But there was more to it than that. I had lost my mother to cancer in April 2007. My husband and brother also were battling cancer at the same time. I am happy to report that they are both survivors. When I met Blondie in September 2007, I was still grieving the loss of my mother. My husband had been out of chemo for only a few months, and my brother had just finished radiation therapy. Blondie came along exactly when I needed her, and she was willing to work with me too.

After four months of training under saddle in Petaluma, Michelle, Frank, and I brought the two-and-a-half-year-old Blondie from Petaluma to Anthony Chabot Equestrian Center. In November 2007, at the age of fifty, I took on the continued training of this beautiful baby. Frank became my mentor throughout this process. Although he had once played professional football for the Oakland Raiders, I think Frank would rather be known as a person who owns, trains, and shows Tennessee Walkers. Now we would both be training Blondie. Frank knew what to do and how to do it, but I was Blondie's rider, so he needed to teach everything to me.

Fortunately, he also had coaching experience and was very patient with me as a willing learner.

We worked three days a week. Each day began with Frank lunging Blondie five minutes in each direction in a round pen. This had been her routine in Petaluma, and we continued it at Chabot. I had some experience free-lunging horses but had never worked with a lunge line. I watched Frank, asked questions, and listened carefully to everything he told me.

After a few weeks, I tried the process myself. I carefully gathered up and held the lunge line in one hand and the lunge whip in the other. Blondie seemed to know I was a rookie. She wouldn't move until I convinced her that I was serious. For a newcomer like me, that meant chasing her around the pen. After ten minutes of that game, it was a toss-up between Blondie and me as to which of us was more winded. Frank assured me that my effort would pay off. As Blondie gained more respect for me, I would secure my place as leader in her herd. Ultimately she would be more responsive when I rode her.

After lunging her, I rode Blondie with the goal of getting her gaiting. Tennessee Walkers have two gaits in addition to the usual walk, trot, canter, gallop, and run gaits most horses have: the flat walk and the running walk. At the flat walk a Tennessee Walker will trot with the front legs and walk with the back legs. The running walk is the same movement, only faster. The result is an extremely smooth ride. It is, however, much easier for the horse to trot than it is to gait. The body position, leg pressure, and reining technique that cued Blondie to begin gaiting were new to me. Equally challenging were the adjustments I had to learn to keep her from trotting instead of gaiting. Since Frank felt he was too tall to ride Blondie, he could use only his words instead of a demonstration to teach me how to ride her at the flat walk and running walk gaits.

I was used to riding well-trained horses and felt nervous with this young horse-in-training. Frank mentored me every step of the way. I began to refer to him as Obi-Wan because of his Jedi-like horse sense. When he observed tension in my body, he assured me that Blondie could feel it also. He explained that a tense rider causes her horse to be anxious too, so I had to consciously release the tension in my body.

Frank taught me the importance of sitting balanced. Blondie confirmed the need for balance because, as a young horse, she tripped a lot. He showed me how using my reins to set her head in the proper position would help her to balance herself and would also be Blondie's cue to begin gaiting. Horses naturally resist having their heads restricted, and Blondie was no exception. But she was smart and quickly understood what I was asking of her. My task was to try to be clear and consistent with my cues. It was me, more than Blondie, who needed training.

November soon gave way to a very cold and wet Northern California winter. By the end of each workout, Blondie and I were soaked, muddy, and exhausted. I gained a deeper understanding of how much I love horses when, knowing I'd come home with frozen limbs, all I could think about was getting up and heading to the barn to work with Blondie.

Michelle came to our training sessions as often as she could and provided needed support, including a videotape of Blondie and me. She gave me horse training books and DVDs so I would have an idea of what we were hoping to achieve. She too shared her considerable knowledge of horses with me. As the months went by, Blondie and I made steady progress. Five months after Frank and I started working together, I rode Blondie in competition at the Monterey Springfest Horse Show. We placed fourth — a respectable ranking among horses and riders with much more training and experience under their belts than Blondie and I had.

Lessons from Blondie

My weekly riding lessons were a constant joy I could count on. I wanted to be able to focus on something besides how cancer had invaded my life. Riding a young horse required my complete concentration. Perhaps that's why I was so willing to participate in Blondie's training.

As only an advanced beginner, I didn't bring any special riding skills to the table. It was hard work in bad weather, and Blondie stumbled from time to time. My husband, ever aware of the occasional mishaps that riders encounter, especially with young horses, gently suggested that I should stop riding for a while.

"You're the only thing keeping our family afloat right now," he said.

"Riding is what's keeping me sane," I replied.

Fortunately, I had sympathetic friends. One day while discussing my latest riding session with a good friend, he suggested that I keep a journal of my work with Blondie. I had never been one to write in journals but I knew there was something special about my time with this horse. So I bought a journal and began writing. I chronicled good and bad days. I tried to find something I had learned every time I rode. What was the lesson of the day?

Soon I began to underline key lessons and accomplishments. I wrote:

- Balance is the key.
- Deep breathing helps with relaxation.
- Sit tall and hold my core.
- Minor adjustments make a big difference.
- Trust that I can do it.

Every now and then, I would go back and read the journal. Then one day it hit me. These were not just lessons in horsemanship; they were life lessons. And Blondie had been my teacher. She was the vehicle through which I learned how to cope with the fear and anxiety that cancer had brought and find strength to keep going. I believe that Blondie is an angel who came to help me through the most difficult time of my life.

Looking back to the first day I had met my angel, I recall the feelings and the question I had asked myself: Is it possible to connect to a horse so thoroughly in one short meeting? My answer is, "You bet." There is no doubt in my mind.

Did Blondie connect with me in the same way? I believe she did. On that first day we met in the pasture, as I faced her and lovingly stroked her shoulder, she curled her neck around my back as if to hug me and say, "I'm here for you too." As time has passed, she continues to let me know her feelings. Yesterday she licked my ear.

MEDITATION

Blondie lured Karen into reconnecting to her childhood love of horses later in life. Is there a horse somewhere who could teach you life lessons?

CHAPTER FOUR

Healing

We've always known that animals make us feel good.
Today, scientific proof is backing up living-room logic
to show that they are actually good for our health.

— MARTY BECKER, DVM

BUTCH, THE HORSE WHO
BELIEVED IN MY DAUGHTER

JODI BUCHAN, *Bemidji, Minnesota*

W hile raising my ten-year-old child, Katie, who has pro-
found mental retardation, my family experienced many
encounters with the two-legged cherubic kind — or what I like
to think of as earthly manifestations of guardian angels. What I
didn't expect to come across was one with four hooves and a
whinny who tucked his Pegasus-sized wings beneath his saddle.

Butch, a retired chestnut gelding, standing about 14 hands
high, was one of the horses at SMaRT, the Snow Mountain Ranch
Therapeutic Riding Program at the YMCA of the Rockies in
Fraser, Colorado, where I took Katie for therapeutic riding. When
corralled in with the mares, Butch would thrust his maleness in the
direction of every potential mate. Since I'm not an equine specialist, I can't say if this was typical behavior, but I came to learn that
Butch was not a typical horse. Whether the mares responded with
a kick or a stampede, he was not deterred. On the other hoof,
whenever he assumed his role as therapy horse, his stride became
patient and gentle. His slow, rhythmic, and repetitive gait and the
natural movement of his hindquarters influenced his riders,
improving their core strength, range of motion, and stamina. It
seemed that whatever his mission, be it misguided mating attempts

or guided therapy activities, wherever his heart led him, Butch's dedication was unflappable.

Butch was not merely the "object of modality," as his purpose is described on paper in grants to funding organizations and reports to medical partners. The breadth of Butch's contribution to the multidisciplinary therapy team, helping clients with movement, communication, and behavior is broader than that of his four-wall office counterparts: the hammock-like net swing and the padded, tubular bolster. These are tools for aiding a therapist in creating positions that strengthen weak neck muscles or challenge balance for their clients, but the net swing and bolster are still inanimate objects. These aids can be useful, even stimulating, but they cannot come close to duplicating the immeasurable benefits of the human-animal bond. By the time midsummer 1997 came around, Butch and my daughter, Katie, had developed an unspoken understanding, a trust between rider and provider.

Katie's Breakthrough

At the beginning of one therapy session, I brought Katie to the base of the wooden mounting ramp. Off in the pine-framed meadow, Rose, the program director, led Butch by the reins. Her golden hair lassoed into a ponytail, Rose led a sun-ripened band of three volunteers who trailed behind Katie and Butch. Katie didn't look directly at any of them. She tipped her head. Using her peripheral vision to briefly glance in their direction, Katie made a guttural note of excited anticipation — her version of language. I held on to Katie's arm as she circled and circled in a jig, similar to what she does when waiting for her school bus to pick her up.

Once Butch was safely between the mounting platform and another elevated wooden base, he stood still and patiently remained with his colleagues. Rose took my daughter up the ramp and guided Katie's hands to the saddle horn. She lifted Katie's right leg over the saddle. A second volunteer, standing on the platform across from Rose, put Katie's foot into a stirrup. When Katie was centered, Rose said, "Katie, tell Butch to walk on."

Katie smiled, unresponsive to Rose's request. Aside from various pitches of sound indicating her excitement or discomfort, Katie's only other form of expressing herself was through an adapted sign language. This was limited to "eat," "drink," and occasionally "more," along with a turn away of her head for "no." We all waited for any kind of response.

Rose repeated the prompt. Katie waited for something to happen, seemingly content just to sit on Butch. Rose waited and repeated the verbal cue a third time. While we listened for any kind of sound from my daughter, the volunteers watched her feet for a slight kicking movement, another way a nonverbal rider could tell Butch she was ready to go.

Finally a volunteer on each side of the horse lifted Katie's feet to help her tap Butch's flanks. Rose spoke for Katie and cheerfully said, "Walk on," and they all headed toward the corral.

Katie's usually curved, slumped posture straightened. She lifted her head and beamed a smile of pride to the audience — me. I swallowed her joy in a lump and claimed it for my own. Katie has had little to say in her own life, and she attempts whatever is asked of her. In spite of significant challenges, she is completely trusting and seems at peace with her circumstances. In that moment I filled with admiration at the way she sat upon Butch. My daughter, my Katie, my Dale Evans.

Engaged in fun and motivated by Butch, Katie didn't recognize that she had been positioned on him to achieve therapeutic goals. They were goals that would help her to walk with more stability, sit and stand with a stronger spine, and engage in developing communication. The fact that the assisted motion of mounting him was the same for getting into the bathtub at home — a specific life skill — was an added bonus. Therapy was boring. Butch was inspiring.

After he walked in the corral, Butch matched his gait to the stride of the volunteer holding his lead rope. The other two volunteers, who were walking on either side for the rider's safety, helped Katie pull back slightly on the reins to stop Butch. They added a "whoa" for her. They handed Katie a plastic ring and guided her hands to drop the ring over a fence post. Next, they wove their path around barrels, stepped over a row of logs, and even turned Katie around to ride Butch backward. Butch was in sync through it all, even to the point of helping to right his rider by giving a little bump of his bum when she started to slide out of position. To offer Katie and Butch a change of scenery, they all headed out to a trail in the woods.

At the end of nearly an hour riding backward, forward, and sideways, Katie's stamina faded. She still smiled but was physically exhausted. As they walked back toward me, before they had even reached a halt, Rose said to me, "Katie said, 'Walk on.'"

"She did?" I asked, a tone of disbelief in my voice.

Katie didn't talk. Ever.

After nine and a half years of occupational therapy, physical therapy, and speech therapy, none of her human therapists had been able to stimulate Katie's language. And none of those synthetic bolsters, dangling net swings, or cause-and-effect toys, which when poked, shaken, or rolled rewarded the effort with a sound, a light, or other stimulus, had prompted any language. In fact, after years of stomped hopes and dreams with words such as, "Maybe when she's three, she'll be able...," "When she's five, eight, ten...," I'd learned to lower my expectations. The fighting with our city and school district for inclusive activities and appropriate services had gotten to me. The words, "Jodi, you can't expect miracles," spoken by a school administrator, had begun to resonate. I'd become half empty. I'd become a mother who thinks of her child, "She can't do that."

Nevertheless, there is something ethereal in therapeutic horseback riding. In spite of her disabilities, Katie was participating in an activity some city slickers find terrifying. She had placed all her trust, vulnerability, and ability in Butch's care without a moment's hesitation.

That very next week on the mounting ramp Rose again told Katie, "Tell Butch to walk on." I could see Butch's left brown eye. His ear twitched backward. I thought I recognized an expression from him of anticipation, of hope.

Then we all heard it — the *w* and *k* sounds were absent. There was no lip closure, but the rhythm and inflection was unmistakable. She said, "Ahh, ann." Butch gently began to walk. He'd heard it. I don't think he ever doubted that he would.

At the end of the session that day, after his biscuit and some TLC, I watched a volunteer lead Butch back into the corral with the rest of the horses. Butch had become the horse who taught me to look up again, who taught me to raise my expectations, to have a little more faith in my daughter's unknown capabilities and future. Butch is the horse who taught me that miracles can happen 14 hands high above the corral dust.

MEDITATION

Butch's belief in Katie brought about a miracle for Jodi to witness. How have horses or other animals listened to your deepest longings and heard what no one else could hear?

VIOLA, WISE MOTHER MARE

❧

TANYA K. WELSCH, *St. Paul, Minnesota*

More than twenty years ago, a unique filly was born in Norway — a Norwegian Fjord Horse named Viola — and began a life representing all that is majestic, soulful, inspiring, and healing in horses. As a Fjord Horse and draft pony, Viola has the typical markings, size, and coloring of the breed that help her stand out in a herd. Her overall color is light tan, called brown dun, and her mane and tail are light cream. The flair comes from a black stripe that runs from the middle of her forelock through the middle of her mane, down her spine and through the end of her tail. As an added bonus, Viola's mane is cut short to stand up, with the black section kept slightly longer. The Fjord breed maintains many primitive markings; Viola has faint horizontal stripes along her knees that carry down to her black hooves. A dark muzzle in a distinct heart-shaped pattern, enclosed in a larger patch of white, extends up the middle of her face. Her striking physical beauty is surpassed by inner beauty that has made her invaluable to the lives of so many children, adults, and horses who have needed her maternal touch.

Viola celebrated her second birthday on American soil in 1988 as she and thirty-nine other Fjords were selected for import to enhance the breed's development. In Fjord circles this horse immigration project was affectionately called "The Big Lift." Settling in upstate New York, Viola took her job as a broodmare very seriously, and it was something she did with excellence. Over the span of thirteen years, she successfully gave birth to ten foals and had the opportunity to remain with one of her daughters to see a grand-foal born. In addition to birthing her own brood, Viola made it known to new horse mothers that she was an expert — and usually an authority figure is not questioned. Much to everyone's surprise, Viola demonstrated her predominantly maternal nature when she decided that another mare's newly born colt would be better raised in her care and attempted to take over mothering duties.

When Viola had reached her mid-teens, she had never had many expectations of herself other than to give birth to foals. She knew how to bully horses in the pasture to get her needs met, and those skills carried over to her relationships with humans. Although accomplished at pulling a plow to work field crops and a sleigh to provide countless hours of pleasure for children and adults during winters in New York, when it came to riding, Viola's training was a source of frustration for those involved. She knew how to move her body in ways that intimidated. It was fairly common for her to slip out from underneath her rider and calmly march herself back to the barn. Everyone agreed that something needed to be done about Viola.

Viola Changes Career Tracks

Realizing that Viola's time as a broodmare was dwindling, her owners decided she needed some professional lessons in ground manners and riding. They placed her with a unique trainer who operated a farm-based program for severely traumatized youth.

Although pregnant with her tenth foal, Viola never hesitated to behave in the same willful fashion at this new barn filled with unfamiliar horses and people. She pushed through doorways, walked away from people when held in halter, and initially had little tolerance for her new training in the Tellington TTouch method — a form of bodywork, ground exercises, and riding that expands a horse's awareness to improve balance, cooperation, and connection.

Tanya's Viola

Wayward behavior aside, Viola was warmly received by many of the children who came to the barn every week to work with the horses. Several young girls took extra measures to care for Viola, citing her pregnancy and that she was the new horse as their reasons for all the attention and fuss. Viola also filled an important program need as a pony-sized mount for youth who were wary of the much taller horses in the barn. Perhaps it was the consistency in her care, the attention to her individual needs outside of being just a broodmare, the structure and routine to her day, or the establishment of parameters and boundaries, but a little after four months from her arrival, Viola began to show others what she had only bestowed upon her babies: sweetness, tenderness, and love.

Viola's time under saddle increased, and she affectionately became known as "the couch with feet" because of her wide girth and back and very steady and even pace. Taken on trail rides with other horses and given an experienced rider, Viola demonstrated less of a barn-sour attitude and willingly engaged with the group. She became a horse one could easily ride bareback and feel a unique connection with her presence, power, and patience. At the

same time, Viola imparted to her rider the importance of awareness, confidence, and responsibility. If her rider was unsure about
direction or gave mixed signals, Viola would exercise her equine
right to stay safe and either stopped until the rider focused or
moved herself and the rider to a place where both could take a
break.

It was Viola's combination of nurturing, ability to learn, and
physical attributes demonstrated during her years as a broodmare
and pleasure horse that helped her fulfill a second career as therapist, teacher, friend, and mentor. In 2003, her owners decided
she had gained sufficient training to qualify for a new, full-time
job. Viola relocated to Minnesota to work with Minnesota Linking Individuals, Nature & Critters (MN LINC), an animal- and
nature-facilitated psychotherapy, learning, and wellness program
for youth and families.

For most people, going to therapy or receiving special education services is uncomfortable and can be wrapped in shame. In
traditional therapy office settings, there is a sense of decorum and
intent that a person is there to talk about things in life that are not
working. It's a time to ask pointed questions, to make difficult decisions, and to face up to fears and concerns. Although those same
aspects are present at the farm, Viola is there to greet clients and
make them feel more comfortable. The environmental atmosphere
and multispecies milieu at MN LINC help clients to physically,
emotionally, and spiritually alter their perceptions of therapy as a
time for probing into painful issues to a more relaxed atmosphere
of wellness, wholeness, and transformation.

Though Viola is a little over 4.5 feet at her shoulders and seemingly formidable in size as a draft pony, people feel an indescrib-
able softness while in her presence. Her look is exotic, with big
brown doe eyes, the heart-shaped shadow around her muzzle, and
her very trendy mane cut in the style of a Mohawk. She stands at

her stall door or pasture gate, ears forward, nickering softly for guests to come and say hello, give her neck a scratch, and possibly offer her an apple or bundle of clover.

Due to her versatility and ability to comfort people's fears about horses, Viola has experienced a similar popularity in her therapy and education work as she did as a broodmare. Her once obstinate behaviors have been transformed into ones that may still have an edge of persistence but are now respectful and slightly comical. She takes her upper lip and, like an elephant, feels people up, sometimes pinching them very gently. Or she softly nudges people when she's been standing with them and wants to get on with her work.

Viola works more easily when there is consistency and listens when there is clarity. These are lessons her clients soon absorb when partnered with her. She will stand her ground when someone needs her strength, and not budge when someone needs her persistence. She has been known to wrap her entire neck and head around clients when they need support, comfort, and nurturance. With her maternal wisdom, Viola helps people address interpersonal struggles by providing them with modeling from an authority figure while also allowing for healing that can come only from the heart and soul of a horse.

Viola and Amy

The year of Viola's first foal also brought the birth of a unique young woman named Amy, and the two were destined to meet when both were in their teens. Life had not always been kind to Amy. She was never sure if she could learn to trust that change is not always traumatic and that there are people and animals in the world who are reliable and would not cause her harm. Her childhood was filled with chaos and provided a breeding ground for inappropriate and dysfunctional behaviors at home, at school, and with others. She had few friends and hung out with peers who considered fighting and stealing to be a standard way to resolve conflict.

Early in high school, Amy became involved in a MN LINC therapy program for teen girls who are survivors of trauma. Amy's love of horses led her mother and therapist to give the program a try. At the time, other means of support were not proving effective. For three years, Amy attended weekly group sessions at the farm and participated in equine-facilitated psychotherapy, for which Viola was one of the main therapists. Together, they began a journey of emotional healing and personal transformation.

Initially, Amy hung back and did not connect with the other girls in the program. Instead, she tried to get her needs for attention met from the staff. When she interacted with Viola, she was stiff, had a difficult time leading, and would easily stumble over her own feet while trying to keep pace with the horse's gait. However, once Amy began some mounted work, an amazing physical change took place: she exemplified equitation posture at its finest. She sat straight and tall, was balanced even riding bareback, and showed little awkwardness in movement. It was as if the freedom of not walking on her own two legs and being carried by a horse's four was providing the stability and groundedness Amy had been looking for since childhood.

In the summer of 2008, Amy's faith in others was tested when Viola needed some time off from doing therapy in preparation for becoming a broodmare one final time. Because of Viola's sensitivity to others and how much she worked from an emotional and spiritual center, I decided to have her take a break from being a therapy horse in an effort to better prepare her for becoming a mother again. Amy's therapists were concerned and wondered how to break the news. Would Amy understand the reason for Viola leaving the group? Would she take it personally and believe that she had done something to cause this change? Would Amy be able to recover and not slide back into old behavior patterns and beliefs?

Outside of her work at the farm, Amy met with her therapists and discussed the change in Viola's involvement with the girls' group. Viola was staying at the farm, so the girls could still see and talk to her when they arrived. A separate time was planned for Amy and others to have individual time with Viola to wish her well. Amy shared that Viola was always with her in dreams and as a form of positive subconscious, telling her she could succeed and be strong. In Amy's inner life Viola also continued to remind Amy just to breathe and that being mindful and present was a continued key to her success. Although losing what had become vital companionship was a difficult transition for her, Amy wrote a letter to Viola and said:

> You are more than a horse to me; you are my very best friend. I started out in group feeling scared and wanting to be perfect. I didn't want to talk about anything or let anyone in. I don't know what it is about you, but something inside me just let go, and I started to share some difficult things in my life. I not only trusted you but I also started to trust everyone in the group. Group is never going to be the same without you, but I am willing to give it a chance with a new horse and new people. You have taught me a lot and so I come to a change in my life. Instead of running, I go with the flow and see what is going to happen next.

Viola's ability to offer subtle life lessons to Amy and other clients is something inherent in her life's role as a mother — a wise mare mentor. Her innate, maternal wisdom touched a part of Amy and helped to heal human wounds. From horse to child, Viola modeled resilience and balance so that when the time was right, Amy could walk on into the next chapter of her life.

Viola, too, has walked on and begun to enter the crone stage of her life, at age twenty-three. Her final breeding did not occur, due to my overwhelming sense that she was no longer interested in being a mother to foals. As she very clearly explained through an animal communicator when asked about her previous breedings, Viola had done her job as broodmare, even though no one ever asked her if that's what she wanted to do. So now we ask and give choices to her, and she continues to be interested in working with people. She no longer works with every youth group program. Her involvement currently includes some individual sessions and more wellness work with adults.

Viola is always present and powerfully calm when she works. She has begun to take on aspects of the ethereal side of life — the impermanence we all have here on Earth and gratitude for what we are given. Even though Viola rarely had a choice in making changes and facing new challenges, she has always embraced her opportunities with courage and authenticity. She has managed to leave a small piece of herself in every heart, so her seeds of wisdom and strength would be ready to grow when her mission for each person was revealed.

MEDITATION

Viola found her calling as mother to both horses and humans. Her role in Tanya's therapeutic program became the catalyst for positive changes. Has a horse or other animal used maternal instincts to help you to heal?

RILEY'S GREATEST GIFT

SALLY HEINS, *Kanab, Utah*

Riley was a gorgeous buckskin quarter horse mare. Her golden coat and striking black markings were enhanced by dapples that gleamed in the sunlight. She had a wonderfully calm and gentle demeanor that allowed her to be trusted with all here at the Best Friends Animal Society sanctuary in Kanab, Utah, where I am a lead vet tech for the Horse Department.

Riley earned her reputation for being trustworthy in a variety of ways. She served as a mentor for a four-month-old miniature horse with a broken leg. She happily nuzzled a young lamb who fought to live while battling a severe joint infection. At more than 1,000 pounds, Riley's immense size seemed irrelevant to her as she cared for these tiny babies. A nurturing soul, she provided affection along with showing gentle boundaries and great maternal instinct.

Riley also demonstrated compelling compassion when one of her companion mares was helped to cross over. On the night that Riley's geriatric friend Ginger had to be euthanized, it was gripping to watch as Riley stood guard, even taking Ginger's lead rope in her mouth and pulling as we worked to save the horse. When our efforts were unable to help, Riley stood vigilantly by her friend's head as the mare lay in the pasture, preparing to cross to a better place. At the very moment the injection sent Ginger on, Riley suddenly ran and kicked her heels. In our minds through this unquestionable display of an animal bond, Riley showed in a breathtaking way her rejoicing that Ginger had been released from her debilitated body and could run free again.

These examples alone are the mark of an exceptional being. However, Riley's distinctiveness went far beyond her exquisite physical beauty and gracious personality.

Riley came to Best Friends from a situation in which she had endured suffering. She arrived emaciated and with an untreated injury. We don't have all the facts, because it happened in the home from where she was removed. The veterinarians determined that Riley likely had torn many tendons in her leg. She walked knuckled over on her fetlock with her hoof curled behind her, giving the impression of broken leg. While no bones were broken, her limb was grossly distorted at the fetlock joint above her hoof.

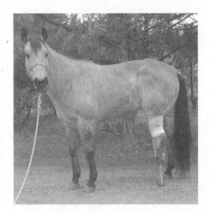

Sally's Riley

Her life at the sanctuary started Riley down a path of healing that spanned almost five years. She was transported to Las Vegas where surgeons removed bone from her leg and attempted to straighten the leg with plates and screws. Despite multiple surgeries and continuous courses of treatment over a period of four years, Riley was still not living with the quality of life that she deserved.

The Best Friends veterinary team and horse department staff, led by Dr. Tara Timpson, DVM, made the decision to have Riley's left hind leg amputated just below her hock. Veterinarians consider this type of aggressive procedure for only ideal equine candidates who have overall good health, strong opposite limbs, an even-tempered demeanor, and financial support to cover extensive veterinary costs. Several factors pointed to Riley being a horse who could benefit from the surgery. She had three sound legs to help endure the adjustment period and was an otherwise healthy and normal middle-aged horse. In addition, Riley had a sensible mentality — she wasn't prone to panicking in unfamiliar situations or while undergoing new treatments. At the sanctuary she would be guaranteed medical care for the remainder of her days.

Most of all, Riley displayed the desire to continue with her life and did not succumb to depression despite challenging situations. Many horses, even those with much lesser injuries, protest bandage changes and other treatments; undergoing them on a regular basis can quickly lead to depression or negative outbursts. Riley was an exception. She did not let her need for continual, sometimes painful, veterinary care cause her to withdraw or become a changed horse. She maintained her gentle spirit and went about her daily life, taking all as it came.

After conscientious deliberation and with optimism, Riley was sent to an equine orthopedic surgeon in Sheridan, Wyoming, for her amputation and to begin a new chapter of her life.

Riley's Missions

To say that being a part of Riley's journey was a learning experience for all of us on her team would be a gross understatement. Riley's true purpose came to life here. She was a teacher. Medically she taught us how to use new equipment and creative procedures. Anatomically she taught her innovative prosthetist how to design a device for a four-legged patient with anatomy and physiology that varied greatly from that of human patients. Publicly she taught numerous visitors and those who followed her story that yes, indeed, "You *can* do that to a horse" and that in appropriate cases you do not always need to euthanize a horse because of a debilitating leg injury.

Riley's story has been featured across the United States and as far away as England and Japan. Her surgeon saw an increase in inquiries and amputation surgeries as Riley helped to spread the word about this bold option. Although the procedure was pioneered in the 1970s, Riley was one of likely less than one hundred horses to have undergone the surgery. The publicity that her story receives is opening minds to exploring options other than euthanasia.

Yet perhaps Riley's greatest teachings were those that can be applied much more broadly. It is rare to witness such displays of courage, tolerance, grace, and trust. She adjusted with impressive intelligence to the mechanics of using a leg that she could not feel while demonstrating courage with each step. Riley showed tolerance during medical procedures and experiences that would agitate almost anyone, horse or human. She maintained her grace through everything from daily bandage changes to media events.

After Riley's prosthetic was taken off, her bandages were changed on a schedule that ranged from twice a day to once every other day. We had a sling that supported Riley when her prosthetic leg was off. However, when she first arrived back at Best Friends four months after her amputation, she stood on three legs for up to thirty minutes while her bandages were changed. The only hint of Riley's anxiousness was a twitch of her eyelid. For the most part she avoided trying to move, kick, panic, or do anything else a typical horse would do in such an unusual situation. She was uneasy, yet she put forth trust in us and maintained her composure, letting on to her true feelings with only that subtle twitch of the eyelid. The twitch would cease when her prosthetic leg was back in place.

Without even the benefit of verbal communication, Riley

accepted all that was put before her. She trusted in the same human species that so horribly failed this determined and elegant creature in her early life.

Riley's journey at this sanctuary of care and compassion was not always along an easy road. There were ups and downs, as we attempted to manage the horse's ever-changing needs, which were as new to us as they were to her. One time Riley sustained an injury while attempting to get up from a nap when she was too close to the stall wall, resulting in decreased nerve function to her front left leg. At that point, Riley was burdened with a left side consisting of an artificial hind leg and a front leg that had decreased sensation at times and caused her to stumble. We began an intensive regimen to treat the injury. Riley showed improvement, but a slight portion of the nerve damage would be permanent. Nevertheless, Riley accepted yet another challenge. She showed determination when executing her daily stretches and walks, as we worked to regain full function in the front leg.

It was telling to step back and realize that often Riley was the one who seemed the most insightfully collected. When we saw Riley struggle, we sometimes felt discouraged. We analyzed and strategized how to overcome a worrisome situation. Often, as we were stressed or anxious, Riley merely waited for the next cookie to be deposited into her adorable mouth. She looked at us as if to say, "Well, come on now, let's get on with it." She lived her life as bravely as possible. It was undoubtedly her purpose to teach us that even rough roads can bear gifts.

Riley's Last Mission

The prosthetic limb gave Riley an additional year of life. On May 12, 2009, two days short of the first anniversary of when she had her leg amputated, perhaps the bravest soul I have ever known was released to the Rainbow Bridge, that fabled place where we meet our animal friends at the end of life. A multitude of complications, including the discovery in her final days of a very large bone spur, led to our no longer being able to manage Riley's pain and provide her with quality of life. Riley was surrounded by those whom she loved as she serenely crossed on, obtaining the true freedom that she deserved. Her passage out of this world was marked with the great beauty and grace we had come to know from this magnificent horse. Although her daily presence would be missed with tremendous sadness, the overwhelming message was how fortunate we all were to have been part of her journey.

I am humbled and have immense gratitude when I think of the impact Riley has had on my life. Aside from being a great patient and beautiful example, she was undeniably a remarkable horse, a teacher, and truly a best friend. To have gained Riley's trust and friendship will forever be one of my most gratifying accomplishments. To have witnessed her resolve in taking life as it comes will forever give me inspiration. I was granted the firsthand opportunity to observe her mission as a teacher and learn from her example. Without question, being Riley's student has been a gift of immeasurable magnitude.

If I was within earshot and spoke to Riley, she would raise her head or perk her ears to listen for my voice; this comfort made me smile every day. She would hold her head perfectly still for me to kiss her forehead. Resting her head against me was an affirmation that she enjoyed being with me. Some of my best times were when I simply sat on the ground next to Riley and talked to her about whatever good or bad I had to share that day. I would leave work in the evenings with Riley standing patiently with her head over the gate, waiting for me to say good night while she bartered for one last cookie from my pocket.

MEDITATION

Who would have thought that Riley's misfortune would have turned into a teaching moment for Sally, the equine health care specialists at Best Friends Animal Society, and other veterinarians around the world? What are the healing gifts for you and others in your life's travails?

SAVED BY MY LI'L MAN

❧

MARY HILL, *Catonsville, Maryland*

I had just received the okay to ride following some minor surgery and couldn't wait to get on my horses. That sunny, crisp
November morning in 1997 marked a month off from riding for
my two quarter horse geldings, Li'l Man, age twenty-five, and
Beau, age eight. Li'l Man, a lovely dark chestnut with white socks
and stockings, was a stout and handsome horse. Beau, a creamy
palomino with platinum mane and tail, was five inches taller than
Li'l Man and had a smooth, elegant gait. They both were full of
extra energy that day.

I had purchased Beau as a lanky three-year-old and managed
to handle his mischievous ways pretty well. I didn't have the same
concerns with Li'l Man, as we had a bond of trust that ran deep
from the day he was born, March 15, 1972. When he was foaled,
Li'l Man had an impacted intestine and had stopped nursing his
mother. We summoned the veterinarian that day, and after treating the hours-old colt with mineral oil down his gullet, he in-
formed me that if the foal didn't pass some manure, he would need
surgery. A friend and I administered soapy water enemas every
two hours through the cold, windy night. Each time I entered his
stall, Li'l Man greeted me at the door as if he knew I was there to
help him. He would lie down while I gathered his neck and head

close to me. He pushed against my body with his face against mine and strained to relieve the impaction. Finally, around 6:30 in the morning, we succeeded in dislodging the blockage, and he was able to start nursing again. Since that rough start, over the years our relationship grew to be strong and steadfast.

Li'l Man seemed to understand my lack of knowledge in many areas of riding and tolerated it just the same. I was young and wanted to get out on the trail and have fun. He always protected me from myself. There were numerous times when he felt that more caution should be exercised and would refuse to continue past strange obstacles or down uncertain pathways. He would slow down or shift when he thought I was unseating myself and help me to regain my balance. I think the most important thing Li'l Man taught me was forgiveness. Horses are so forgiving, forgetting your bad moods, your youthful ignorance, or even stupidity. As I matured, I began to realize what forgiving means and how important it was to one's spiritual well-being.

I knew that on my first day back after recovering from surgery I would need most of my energy to deal with the younger horse. I left Li'l Man loose in the pasture because he never caused a problem while I was working his stable mate. In fact, sometimes he would follow along, and I could work both horses simultaneously. With lunge line in hand I went out on a flat area of the pasture sixty to seventy yards from the paddock.

As I walked to the working area, I remembered what my husband had said before I left the house that morning: "Be careful and don't do anything stupid." Normally, I would throw the line behind me so as not to risk stepping in the coil. In an effort to be extra cautious, I instead did what some of my friends had suggested as a technique. I coiled the twenty-five-foot line in one hand while using the lunge whip in my opposite hand.

About five minutes into the warm-up with Beau, my neighbor's tractor began to backfire repeatedly. It spooked my 16-hand, 1,200-pound gelding, who already was showing his exuberance. At five feet, three inches tall and weighing 115 pounds, I was clearly no match for Beau's strength and power. With what felt like the force of a freight train, he pulled me so fast and hard that I thought my arms would be ripped from their sockets. The lunge line whizzed through my hands. I barely had an instant to realize what was about to happen. I had stepped into the coil. One of my worst nightmares was coming true. Instantly I was slammed to the ground with the line pulled tightly just below my left knee.

Quarter horses can reach top speed in four strides. I struggled to grab the line. My right leg freewheeled, banging the ground as Beau dragged me. My body twisted, and I continued to struggle. Within only a couple of seconds, I had to surrender to the inevitable and go limp, certain that my life was over.

Somewhere in my numb consciousness, I heard Li'l Man shrieking again and again. Then I felt the speed at which Beau was dragging me slow down. I lifted my head to see Li'l Man running back and forth in front of the paddock gate. He continued to shriek at the top of his lungs. Thank God, Beau heeded his call and turned away from the gate area. There were two or three partially submerged timbers in place at the gate to keep stone dust from running off in heavy rains. If my head had hit those timbers, I most certainly would have suffered a devastating injury, maybe even death.

Li'l Man slowly drove Beau down and away from the gate area and timbers. He kept driving him until Beau stopped twenty yards or so into the pasture. All I could think of in my scrambled head was to get the line off my leg as quickly as possible before Beau took a notion to travel again.

I looked bleary-eyed at Beau's expression. I could tell he was horrified as he stared back at me sitting on the ground. Beau's fright and flight had rendered him oblivious to me or anything else except my wise old gelding who now stood in front of him. Beau froze as if he didn't know what to do next. Li'l Man must have also realized Beau hadn't meant to hurt me. He lowered his head and slowly approached Beau, gently nickering that it was time for the excitable horse to calm down.

Mary and Li'l Man

I thanked God that I was still alive and Li'l Man for making my survival possible. The vision in my left eye blurred. My right leg hurt. I managed to get up and limp over to Beau. I couldn't find my cell phone, so I hobbled to the farm owner's house to get help. The owner was a retired orthopedic surgeon who allowed me to keep my horses at his seven-acre farm bordering the state park. Over the years that I had boarded my horses with him, he'd given his professional opinions and help whenever he could. But neither he nor his wife was at home. Fortunately the door was unlocked, which meant they were out on a short errand.

I used their kitchen phone and called my friend Jean, who lives nearby and is a registered nurse. The conversation went something like this:

"Jean, are you babysitting?"

"No," she replied.

"Do you think you could take me to the hospital?"

Jean didn't even stop to ask what had happened. She hung up and left home immediately, arriving as I was attempting to unsaddle Beau. Later, she said that her first impression of me was that I looked like a woman who had originally dressed in black, but everything had been transformed to muddy brown except my left leg, which had been lifted above the ground on my trip across the pasture.

In the hospital everyone began calling me the muddy lady. I felt badly for the chunks of mud and dirt that followed my trail from examination area to X-ray and back. My right ankle needed reconstruction. The tendons and ligaments were torn, and I had a broken tibia. Also, the accident had torn cartilage in my knee and sprained ligaments. To top it off, I had a swollen, completely closed black eye.

I had surgery in November on the day before Thanksgiving and didn't return to work until early February. I was especially thankful that Thanksgiving for having been spared death or injuries that could have rendered me partially or wholly disabled.

In my heart I believe that Li'l Man saved my life that day. This moment in time, this single act of courage, compassion, and love fulfilled the most important purpose in his life. He was my soul mate, my guardian, my friend. From the day we bred his dam to the moment I placed my hand on his mother's womb and felt his heartbeat to his birth in March 1972 to the day in June 2008 when he and I looked into each other's eyes and surrendered him to Heaven, we thought and acted as one. Wherever we went, for more than half my life, he protected and taught me so much. He was and always will be my angel horse, my Li'l Man.

MEDITATION

Li'l Man wasn't about to let his best friend Mary lose her life to a spooked horse. How have animals saved you from life-threatening situations or emotional meltdowns?

CHARLIE,
THE WHITE MARBLE STATUE HEALER

MEAGHAN MARTIN, *Hollis, Maine*

In the winter, horseback riders in Maine are allowed by the town of Scarborough to trailer the horses to Pine Point Beach and ride as long as we have a current permit from the town. One year my friend Emily and I went to the beach with Charlie, my seven-year-old white-gray Standardbred gelding, and Camelias (Cam), my twenty-five-year-old Standardbred mare.

After Emily and I spent a couple of hours galloping on the sand with Charlie and Cam, jumping driftwood logs, and playing in the water, we brought the horses back to the trailer. We untacked them and decided to hand-walk them on the beach to cool off and roll in the sand, if they wanted to. I had been riding Charlie, but since Emily and I still had on our helmets, we decided to switch horses so that I could ride Cam. I handed Charlie to Emily, and she gave me a boost onto Cam's bare back.

We stopped and spoke to people here and there, enjoying the fifteen or twenty minutes before we had to leave the beach. I noticed a woman watching our horses carefully. She was of Asian descent, with braided midnight-black hair wound beautifully around her head. I made eye contact with Emily, and she nodded. She, too, had seen the woman observing our horses.

We approached the woman and asked if she would like to meet the horses. Instead of speaking to us, she did sign language, and we realized the woman was deaf. She motioned toward her husband, who was aiming a questioning glance at us, and their two dogs. We nodded to her, and she waved her husband and dogs in our direction.

The woman was able to read lips and speak to an extent. She managed to ask Emily what Charlie's name and age were. After silently greeting Charlie she asked Emily, "Therapy horse?" Emily replied, "No, he is just a really good boy." The woman smiled and moved toward Cam.

Meaghan's Charlie

Usually Cam is the horse people are drawn to, with her kind, wise mahogany brown eyes and mellow disposition. But the woman remained with Cam and me only long enough to ask Cam's name and age. She smiled and stroked Cam's nose for a moment but then went straight back to Emily and Charlie.

Charlie is young and goofy and has an engaging personality, but he is certainly not the type of horse to stand still for hugs and kisses. Usually he pulls away and sends a dirty look to any giver of affection. Perhaps, though, that woman needed Charlie, and he knew it. What Charlie did that day was something I have never seen him or any horse do.

When the woman went back to Charlie, she began stroking his neck before wrapping her arms around him in a loving embrace. He stood, like a white marble statue, as the woman rested her face on his neck. Instead of moving away, Charlie turned his head to look at the woman and nuzzled her gently. He wrapped his head around her entire body and stood perfectly still.

Waves crashed behind us, and gulls swooped through the air, their cries sounding over the din of pounding waves. An expression of pure peace and happiness lit the woman's face. In that moment, the world became silent, and time stood still. Nothing else mattered. By the time she released her arms from Charlie's neck, tears had filled her eyes. Over and over again, the woman signed "Thank you" to me. Then she, her husband, and two dogs walked away from us as silently as they had come.

I knew we were on the beach that day for a reason. Maybe it was so that this beautiful woman could meet Charlie and have a moment of connection with him. Charlie understood her in a world where she must have felt like so few could. Horses change lives. They reach out to people who may not trust humans. They heal broken spirits, they heal broken people, and they heal broken hearts.

MEDITATION

Charlie understood that the deaf woman needed his love and attention. While Meaghan watched the startling encounter unfold, she knew she was in the presence of something much greater than herself, or even of her horse. When have you been blessed with the gift of healing at a moment you least expected it?

CHAPTER FIVE

Bringing Joy and Hope

*Love is patient and kind; it is not jealous or conceited
or proud; love is not ill-mannered or selfish or irritable;
love does not keep a record of wrongs; love is not happy
with evil, but is happy with truth. Love never gives up;
and its faith, hope, and patience never fail.*

— 1 CORINTHIANS, 13:4–7

CHEVY'S COMPASSION

❧

SHEILA ANDERSON, *Wellington, Colorado*

Many years ago, I went on a mission to find the perfect horse for reining. As soon as I expressed interest in a purchase, my trainer found me OB San Jose, aka Chevy. He is a light palomino Appaloosa with a huge blanket, silky white mane and tail, and the most beautiful amber eyes. An unassuming horse, he's barely taller than the standard size for a pony but built wide and tough like a truck. That's how he got his nickname, Chevy. When I rode him, it was like riding in a finely tuned sports car. All the bells and whistles were there, and he handled like a dream. I bet everyone, including my husband, knew by the look on my face that this was the horse for me. We had agreed I had spent enough on horses, but this one was special. So out came the checkbook, and Chevy was on his way to my barn.

I was so excited when the trailer carrying Chevy pulled up to my barn — that is, until the door opened. The first thing that concerned me was that the horse was hobbled in his trailer. It's hard enough for a horse to safely stand in a moving trailer, but hobbles prevent them from spreading their legs for stability, as the truck bounces around. I asked his former owner, who was delivering him, why the hobbling was necessary. She explained that Chevy would kick off the shoes on his back feet and cause hoof damage if she didn't hobble him in the trailer. I knew this wasn't acceptable and was more than willing to help him learn to ride in a trailer without harming himself.

Within the first month of ownership, I discovered my perfect horse had many problems. Chevy would furiously kick the walls inside his stall, especially around feeding time. Sometimes he would cast himself in his stall, which meant serious trouble. Horses are said to cast themselves when they lie down and roll around in the clean shavings in the confined space of their stall and accidentally roll their legs tightly against the wall. Then they are not able to turn back over or get up on their own. The weight and stress they put on their organs from struggling to get free from this position causes serious illness, injury, or death. Chevy cast himself so often that we began to think he was doing it on purpose.

Then there was the fact no one could touch Chevy's face from above the nose to the middle of his neck. We guessed it had something to do with the numerous scars on his ears, although we didn't know how he had gotten them. In addition, he hated needles, so it was hard to vaccinate him.

Emotionally, Chevy remained distant. This horse was like a well-trained soldier. He showed no feelings and would avoid eye contact. I admit that after only three months owning him, I was disappointed. My perfect horse was not so perfect. Over the next year, I gradually realized all the challenges Chevy would present. His vices were dangerous to him and held us both back from doing well in the reining shows. More important was Chevy's well-being. Something in his past was causing him to react this way, and I had to get him through it. This time, he had someone who believed in him and would help overcome his problems, sticking by him for the long haul.

Befriending Chevy

I decided I wanted an all-around happy horse, so I didn't attempt to show Chevy at the reining shows in Ocala, Florida, for the next few months. Instead, I made our rides fun. Within just four months, trail rides became something he grew to enjoy. Hours of my touching and playing with him proved to him that he could trust me. Soon I was able to touch his face, eyes, and ears without any negative reaction.

Sheila and Chevy

I made him love the trailer by taking his shoes off. Now he wouldn't hurt himself if he kicked while being transported. Plus, we took short fun trips with him instead of the four-hour rides to the reining show. Working cows was something he enjoyed, so we did it as often as possible. He simply had to move cows from one pen to the other or separate a calf from the herd for vaccines or branding. Sometimes we would trailer to an open meadow, so he could eat fresh grass. I turned him out in an open field instead of in a stall, so he could do what he wanted. Things were becoming enjoyable for him, and his initial problems began to fade.

Chevy came around slowly, but he came around. He started to show affection toward me by nuzzling my hair or softly laying his head on my shoulder. Placing a bridle on him or touching his head was no longer an issue. He trusted me. When he was in the pasture, he would run to the fence to see me. He no longer kicked in the stall or trailer. I loved riding him more than ever, because he was paying close attention to my cues or commands. He tried to do what I wanted, and he was happy when we were training. Now he had become the horse I had dreamed of, and our relationship kept improving.

Chevy and I began to form a bond unlike I'd had with any horse. I knew the moment it happened. I was sitting in the meadow in front of him as he grazed. He softly nuzzled the top of my head, gently putting my hair in his mouth and smelling the back of my neck. He half-closed his eyes and stayed there for several minutes. Time stopped, and we just enjoyed the warm sunshine and soft breeze together. I knew then that he and I had become best friends. This sign of affection became the regular way he showed that he cared.

All Chevy's attitude and behavior problems had melted away. He started giving me 150 percent at every show. OB San Jose aka Chevy became a two-time bronze trophy Working Cow Horse winner with the National Reined Cow Horse Association. The Working Cow Horse competition combines the thrill of cutting with the finesse of reining, and Chevy excelled at it. He earned points in the Appaloosa Horse Club in both halter and reining. He earned more than $3,000 in reining in the National Reining Horse Association as well as numerous titles and awards through the Florida Reining Horse Association.

Chevy's Decision

Chevy was polite and affectionate, careful and protective, especially on the trails. When I rode him I could look in the direction I wanted to go, and he would follow. I could relax in the saddle and he would stop. I could turn him loose camping, and he would stay with me. He would move back under me if I began to fall. He was careful not to bump into me or step on my feet when I was next to him. He was always gentle, kind, and patient. It wasn't that I helped him overcome his vices; it was that he taught me to communicate better and be more understanding.

Chevy's good behavior earned him a special treat — friends and I would meet for trail rides with Chevy and their horses on a 6,000-acre preserve. On one ride in late August, unfortunately for us, the ground was still wet. We got stuck in the middle of swamp conditions after we lost our trail. Mosquitoes were everywhere, and we had to run back to camp to avoid the swarm. By the time we returned, we were covered with bites. But all in all, it was a good ride on my great horse.

Not more than a week passed, and I noticed one morning that Chevy had some lameness in his rear leg. By evening he was severely lame in both hind legs and running a fever. I called our veterinarian, Dr. Mike Carinda, DVM. He thought Chevy might have contracted West Nile virus from the mosquito bites on the swampy trail ride. It was October 2001, and vaccine for West Nile virus, a rare strain of encephalitis, was only available in very limited quantity. In any case, it was too late for Chevy to be vaccinated.

We rushed Chevy to the Wellington Equine Associates in Florida, where he was hospitalized. When tests came back positive for West Nile virus, Chevy's became the first confirmed case in Broward County. The Florida State Veterinarian, someone from the Florida State Health Department, and news crews hurried to the hospital. This was a major health concern, because horses and birds are an indicator species of the West Nile virus, and they contract it before it starts appearing in humans. The Department of Health now had to spread warnings through the media to educate the public.

Chevy's symptoms grew from worse to awful. Within days, he developed pneumonia. His rear legs were nearly paralyzed. His body bowed to the left in the shape of a banana. He held himself up by the wall of his hospital barn stall and couldn't lie down. He had no night vision and could barely see during the day. The pain he was in made him sensitive to light.

Next, his mouth became paralyzed, and he drooled so much that he couldn't eat or drink. We kept him alive with IV fluids. He could no longer control his reflexes. Any sudden noise caused him to jump or jerk so violently that he would nearly fall over. He stared ahead blankly, leaning on the wall in severe pain. My vets, Dr. Carinda and Dr. Ben Schachter, DVM, were doing all they could. The disease had been caught early, but in fewer than seven days Chevy looked nothing like the stunning show horse I loved so much.

Finally the day came when I had to make the decision whether or not to euthanize Chevy. I went into his stall one last time to see my poor friend. He didn't seem to recognize me and was not able to respond to anything. He looked as if he was gone already, and his suffering had become unbearable. Still, the pain of this decision was too much for me. I wrapped my arms around my knees and sat on the stall floor in a heap of emotion, sobbing uncontrollably.

I heard some rubbing noise but was too upset to look up. Then a large blob of drool dripped down onto my forehead. At first, I felt a thump on my head by Chevy's lower, drooping lip bumping me too hard. After he got the reflex jerking motion under control he tried again and softly placed his muzzle on my head. As he had done so many times before, with his upper lip, he ever so gently nuzzled my hair and tried to take a piece of it in his mouth. But his lower lip was still paralyzed. He had used the wall of his stall to move his half-paralyzed body closer to me. Worn out by this effort, he rested his head in my hands and let out a soft sigh. I held up a small handful of hay, and he took it. In an effort to simply please me, he ate it.

Over the next few days I stayed with Chevy as much as possible. It wasn't just that I loved him. It was that we loved each other, and he was my best and most trusted friend. He showed me he still had life in him, and I would now try to repay some of the great things he had done for me. No matter what he needed, I would make sure he had it. Along with the amazing staff at the hospital, I helped with his supportive care. The only time he would eat or drink was with me present until he was well enough to go home.

At home Chevy continued to improve. After a year of being out in the pasture and healing, Chevy was back to normal.

Before this experience, I had never realized how deeply compassionate an animal can be. Chevy had a swollen brain. He was in pain beyond anything most of us have gone though. Horses are herd animals and have a strong instinct to stay on their feet when injured or ill. It must have been an extreme challenge for him to remain standing on his half-paralyzed legs for days. By the time Chevy nuzzled my head in the stall on that fateful day, he must have been exhausted. He could hardly see, noise nearly drove him mad, and he couldn't eat. With all that to deal with, he'd made the supreme effort to comfort me. Not because I was wounded or sick. Just because I was sad. To some, his gesture of affection might seem small, but to a horse who was so very sick it was a huge task.

That day, Chevy put himself last and showed concern for me when clearly he was the one who needed it more. With a simple gesture he gave me the ultimate gift and showed me how blessed I am to be loved so deeply by a creature I admire above all else

Because of Chevy's patience and understanding, I became a better mother to my kids. I showed them that I cared a lot more than I had. I was a better friend because I listened more. I understood that sometimes a person, or a horse, just needs someone to believe in them. Chevy showed me that a true friend is there for you no matter what. He taught me we could overcome our past through trust. I learned never to give up and that I can get through any roadblocks life throws at me by standing tough. Most of all, Chevy proved that having even one thing to live for makes life worth living.

MEDITATION

Chevy gave service not only to Sheila but also to others who needed hope that West Nile virus wasn't always fatal. How have horses imparted hope to you?

TRAVELING TO THE PLACE
ON PEEN'S BREATH

❧

PAULINE PETERSON, *Farmington, Minnesota*

P een is my youngest Morgan mare. Her full name is Paupeen, which is what my younger brothers called me before they were old enough to pronounce Pauline. Peen is not very tall, at only 14.2 hands. She is black, but the summer sun bleaches her hair to brown. Her head is very feminine with perfectly proportioned ears. Her body is balanced equally into thirds, with her head and neck the first third, her barrel or middle section the second third, and her hips and rear end the last third. Looking like a beautiful woman with long hair, Peen tosses back her forelock, the forehead hair. The only white on her is a star on her forehead, shaped like a tilted letter z.

On a cold winter day, I had brought Peen out of her pasture and into the barn where I board my horses near Welch, Minnesota. I had not ridden her for a long time. I wanted to comb out all the fairy twirls that had tangled her unsightly mane. There is a legend that at night, fairies ride horses in the pasture and hang on to them by twisting and twirling the horse's mane. I intended to undo what the fairies had done.

Peen has always fussed when I have tried to comb her mane. Most horses love to have this done, but not her. I was trying to figure out how to groom her without losing my patience. As we stood in the cement aisle, I attached each of the long crosstie ropes, connected to vertical beams on opposite sides of the aisle, to her halter. I had sprayed hair conditioner on her mane and started to comb the ends and work up toward the crest of her neck.

She still fussed by turning her head and banging my arm with her nose. She bit the comb in my hand. She sidestepped and pushed. Then I remembered that Peen likes to exchange breath with me. Animals do this to each other sometimes.

I stopped combing and stood directly in front of her. She immediately put her nose to my face and rapidly moved her upper lip from side to side against my nose. Then her lip was still, and she inhaled my breath deep into her body. Her exhale covered me with warm, sweet breath. With her next inhaled breath, I felt as if she was absorbing my whole being. She blew into my left ear. My, that felt good.

Slowly I moved to her left side, and she followed me. Her lips stayed connected to my left ear. I began gently combing her mane. She became very quiet. I grew more relaxed, releasing any idea of trying to control her. I matched my breathing to the rhythm of hers.

In an instant I lost all boundaries of my body and seemed to travel to a place that I had never been to before. Or had I? I felt connected to everything and everywhere in the universe all at once. Time disappeared. I no longer felt separateness. I became a drop of water falling back into the ocean and remembering that I was already part of the sea. I transcended galaxies with no pain, no anxiety, and no boundaries. Peen and I melted into the sublime unity of everything.

Then as quickly as the experience happened, it changed. I recognized the hard feel of the cement underneath my feet. I again felt Peen's breath in my left ear. A stallion whinnied at the other end of the barn. I heard scraping sounds of men cleaning it while they talked to each other. As my eyes refocused, I realized that goose bumps had appeared on my arms. Tears sprang to my eyes. Overwhelmed with the sensations I had experienced and feeling ecstatic joy, I became embarrassed. I tried to take some deep breaths and compose myself.

I looked around and had the impression that everything seemed surrounded by a glow. Sparkles twinkled in my peripheral vision. I wasn't sure who I was. The only sense that grounded me in the world again was the smell of Peen's sweet breath. I slowly returned to combing her mane. Peen straightened out her neck and lowered her head, a sign of total relaxation. I remained present in the moment and finished grooming her.

Pauline's Peen

Later that day, I rode on the trail atop Peen's mother, Kayla, who is much bigger than Peen. She's a traditional picture of massive, powerful femininity, dressed in black with a nicely arched Morgan neck, huge chest, and matching rear end that sways with each step. The trail Kayla and I were on wound through a wooded, thickly covered ring of leafy trees that surround huge corn or soybean fields. It snakes along the Cannon River, which winds around an island. On our side of the river bottom, the land is flat, while bluffs border the other side. It usually takes Kayla and me more than an hour to make the circuit, at a walk, down the valley and back to the barn.

As Kayla and I rode, I pondered the experience I'd had with Peen at the barn and mulled over thoughts and questions about it. I have gone before to this place of being everywhere all at once, but only after a long meditation. This time, my young horse seemed to be a bridge to the experience and had triggered my spiritual journey. Maybe my willingness to join with her on her terms by exchanging our breaths had started it. Was our journey together her mission for me that day?

Then, in my mind, I asked Kayla about my experience with Peen by posing the question: Could the Holy Spirit possibly be black, female, and equine? Kayla would know the answer because we have connected spiritually in the deepest of ways. I had seen her in a dream before we first met, making her literally my dream horse. Over the years our relationship had become very close. Although most mares give birth when no one is around, Kayla had let me be present to witness and help deliver her first foals. We had bonded deeply when she had become critically ill a month before her foaling date. I had stayed with her for days, praying, crying, massaging her, and giving her the antibiotics. Because of our closeness, I often talk with her in my mind and out loud. In answer to my question that day, I heard Kayla chuckle and say, "You think you have to understand everything, don't you?"

Kayla's reply made me realize I simply needed to accept and enjoy, not question and analyze the gift of spiritual traveling that Peen had given to me. Peen, my perfectly precious mare, had taken as her mission to join her breath with mine and lift me into a place of peace and wonder. Her mother taught me that all I had to do was accept that I had been blessed.

MEDITATION

The moment of grace between Pauline and Peen brought Pauline to a place of ecstatic joy. Has the breath or presence of an animal transported you to heavenly heights?

ASLEEP WITH SAKI

❖

SAM YOUNGHANS, *Glendale, California*

I first met Saki while living on a 168-acre ranch in the mountains north of Sonoma, California. One day, while driving through the valley, I saw a number of horses standing in a small field near a sign that said, "Horses for Sale." My wife, Paula, and I pulled into the drive and walked to the field to get a better look at the horses. A bay quarter horse mare about 16 hands tall caught my eye. She had a white mark on her forehead and one white boot on her right leg. She stood still among the other horses, who backed away as I approached them, as if they were making way for me.

When I was close enough, the horse nuzzled me. I rubbed her head and neck and felt a strong feeling of friendship toward her. It was love at first sight. I felt as though we had been friends from another life and were connecting again. I grew up with dogs and horses, so I have always treated animals with love and respect and felt that we communicated with each other.

While the owner saddled the horse, I overheard quiet comments from some of the people who were milling around the corral. I couldn't make out the words, but their actions conveyed that they knew something about this horse. I told Paula I had a clue that I would have an interesting ride.

I was right. The horse started bucking before I had my right foot in the stirrup. I stayed on for three-quarters of the corral, and then she threw me. But I knew we were meant for each other and felt certain that I could gentle and ride her, so I bought her anyway. I named her Saki, after the Japanese rice wine, saki, because she seemed both sweet and spirited.

Saki was to be delivered the following day. In order for the two of us to get to know each other, I met the horse trailer at the foothills of the ranch and took delivery there. I walked Saki about three and half miles up the mountain road. To reach the barn and house, it was necessary to go through the vineyard and then down a winding road. The vineyard was fenced and gated, so I planned to try to ride Saki there. I figured she might be friendlier and a little tired after that long walk, and it would be a good time to get on her.

I saddled her with an old western saddle that had been on the ranch for a long time. The saddle didn't have a belly cinch, so I used the strap that was with it. Paula watched us and told me that I'd placed the saddle a foot above Saki's back. I positioned my feet above the saddle, and of course, Saki would have none of this. She wasn't a bit tired and tossed me so that I landed on the ground. I tightened the strap on the saddle and tried again, only to fly off once more. The ground in the vineyard was soft, so it was a good place to land.

After three attempts, I decided I'd better gentle Saki before I ruined her or she ruined me. When horses have never been ridden, they object to any weight on their backs. Cowboys call riding a bucking horse until it gentles down "breaking" the horse, but I didn't want to break her spirit. I walked the horse down to her new home.

Every day I put the saddle on Saki's back and began the process of neck-reining her before attempting to ride her again. Western-style riding guides a horse by using pressure on the neck with the reins, called neck-reining, as opposed to English style, which guides a horse by pulling on the reins. With the bit and bridle we'd walk around the ranch, using the reins as if I was mounted. While guiding Saki around the ranch in this manner, I talked to her and rubbed her neck.

Then one day a friend came to visit with his buddy who was a cowboy. The cowboy said he would show me how to break Saki. I don't like that term because it implies harsh treatment. He told me to attach two sacks full of dirt to her saddle and a long rope to her halter. I did this with reservations, because Saki and I were getting along very well. However, the cowboy was very convincing, and I went along with him, thinking maybe it wouldn't be too severe.

As soon as the weights touched Saki's sides she took off, bucking, trying to throw the load. The cowboy dropped the rope before I could get to it, and Saki jumped a five-strand barbed wire fence and took off. I swore I would never allow that kind of treatment again. Saki had shown me her wonderful spirit, and I was not about to break it.

This happened about a month after Saki came up the mountain to the ranch, so she was familiar with the area and didn't run far. As a matter of fact, after my friend and the cowboy left, she returned to one of the vineyards just above our house. She was chewing on some grass; I walked up to her and apologized. I could tell she understood and was happy to see me alone. I took the reins and brought her back down the hill to the barn and some hay. Saki forgave me. The next day, we returned to our old routines.

I continued to give Saki love and trust, and she returned it. By now, it had been more than three months since she had become part of our lives. I never locked her in. Saki was free to roam around the ranch or go into her stall in the barn. I knew she would not run away; although, to catch her, a bag of oats always helped.

One day, we were ambling together up the winding, narrow gravel road toward the vineyard. I got the feeling that the time was right to climb into the saddle. Saki accepted me, and we walked around the ranch. Our first ride together brought a wonderful feeling to be sitting in the saddle and letting her take me up the road. I felt that she enjoyed it also. When we got back to the barn, I gave her a nice bucket of oats. After that night, we rode every day, all over the ranch and the surrounding area, and we were getting to know each other.

About a week after our first suc-cessful ride, I came home from work at 10:30 at night. In this area around Sonoma, referred to as "the valley of the moon," with the full moon shining down on me as I drove through the vineyard, it seemed almost like day-time. The only thing on my mind was how much I would enjoy taking a moonlight ride with Saki.

Sam and Saki

When I reached home, I grabbed some oats, caught Saki, saddled her, and we had a delightful ride around the ranch. Then we rode up the winding road to the top and into the vineyard. It was a grand feeling that we shared. But I didn't realize how much it had affected her until later that night. When we returned, I took off Saki's saddle and bridle and turned her loose.

I went into the house and joined Paula, who was watching tel-evision. During a commercial I went into the kitchen to get a drink of water and heard a noise at the kitchen door window. It was Saki, looking in at me with her nose against the glass. She seemed so lonely that I told Paula I was going to visit with Saki for a while.

I took a sleeping bag and threw it on the slightly sloping

ground between the house and the barn. The moon lit the calm and peaceful area. No city lights hid the stars; no noises broke the beautiful silence. Saki watched me come out of the house and then she snorted. I greeted her and said that I would keep her company for a while. Then I crawled into the sleeping bag.

What happened next was not a dream. She stood over me and started pulling on the sleeping bag with her teeth. I usually had to coax her with oats to come near me, but that night, I had to chase her off. She walked away, and I began to doze.

I awoke to the sound of hooves passing just above my head. It was Saki walking by me. She edged down the slope so that her rump faced me. I thought she might be getting ready to kick me out of the sleeping bag and got ready to roll.

Instead of kicking me, Saki laid beside me with her hooves facing down the slight slope, her rear near me, and her head level with mine. She was so close that I was able to reach out and pat her on the rump. She lifted up her head, looked back at me over her shoulder, gave a slight whinny, and then laid her head back down. At that moment I felt an overwhelming love, a feeling that is hard to describe, rush through me. Saki had accepted me. Saki and I slept side by side, or rather with her rump by my side. As I dozed off, the thought occurred to me that if anyone asked if I had ever slept with a horse, I would have to answer, "Yes, and very soundly."

Twenty years later, when I was living in Hollywood, I met Ben Johnson, the actor in many of the John Wayne western movies. I told him this story and he said, "Sam, that's the doggondest horse story I ever heard."

Saki taught me many things over the years about love and caring. That same year my son was born, and when he was five, he rode Saki. I believe Saki helped me become a caring father to all my children. Saki lived to be twenty-one years old. I know we will meet again in the universe, and maybe Saki will gentle me.

MEDITATION

Funny as it is to visualize Saki sleeping side by side with Sam, there is a tenderness to this story that touches the heart. Has a horse given you the joy of laughter?

CHEROKEE TOOK WING

BARBARA FENWICK, *Carberry, Manitoba, Canada*

On what was quite possibly the saddest day of my life, the sky still was blue, the birds sang, poplar tree leaves fluttered in the gentle afternoon breeze. It was a beautiful July morning in 2004.

I moved robotically, doing chores and watching the clock. Cherokee, my sixteen-year-old buckskin-colored Appaloosa with beautiful brown polka dots on his rump and tons of personality remained peacefully in the barn. As I walked the short distance from my house to get him, the other horses followed. Perhaps they were wondering what was up, or maybe they already knew. Why was I feeding them this time of day? "There must be something wrong," they might have been thinking.

Cherokee didn't seem to question my motives even though I wasn't serving his regular diet. While he greedily ate the huge feed of oats and a double-sized feeding of sweet alfalfa hay I had dished out for him, it seemed that his only focus was on the food.

While Cherokee ate, in the distant pasture I could hear the tractor working. Not a comforting sound. An hour later the sound of a truck engine made my heart climb higher into my throat. It was time.

I led Cherokee and his best friend, my spotted Tennessee Walker horse, Spirit, out to pasture. We stopped on the crest of a small hill, one that was well secluded and chosen with care. The truck climbed the hill and parked.

Wayne, our local veterinarian, stepped out into this beautiful day. Our good friend and neighbor, Dave, had stopped his tractor a few yards away and now stood beside his pickup truck with his old dog, Sam, nearby. Dave had finished digging the huge hole. It would fit a horse. My husband, George, stood with the two other men. Each of us in our own way prepared to deal with and accept what we were there to do.

I would take my last walk with Cherokee down into the giant hole and say good-bye to the horse who was really too young to die but had suffered long enough. I had bought Cherokee as a three-year-old. We had incredibly great times together for nine years until I became aware that I could not ride trotting horses anymore because of problems with my back and neck. Due to my physical situation and the fact that I now owned and bred Tennessee Walking horses, Cherokee was not getting ridden much anymore. A local resident had expressed interest in buying him. Cherokee was a horse with much stamina, so I decided to let him go to a new home where he could get out and enjoy companionship and trails again. The man assured me that Cherokee would be well cared for and have a good, active future.

It didn't happen. I would see Cherokee in the man's pasture when I passed by the farm where he lived. He wasn't being ridden much at all. As time went on, I saw signs of him receiving minimal attention or care. A combination of poor quality feed and not maintaining his health or hoof care was taking its toll.

One spring day, two years later, I stopped along the road and went over to have a good look at Cherokee. I cried. He was a mess. His breathing was labored, and his feet were so incredibly long that he could hardly walk. I should never have sold him. He would have been better off being a pasture ornament at my ranch than ending up like this. I knew that I had to get him out of there. I finally persuaded the owner to sell him back to me. So began our last two years together.

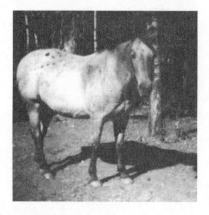

Barbara's Cherokee

Cherokee was never going to be sound again, but I wanted to help him be comfortable, however long his life lasted. His foundered feet could no longer carry him happily across the pastures. His lungs, which had been damaged from heaves, a bronchial disease, made each breath labored and painful. Special shoeing and pads and medication for pain and to aid his breathing helped for a while. Then the pain became so unbearable that we could no longer shoe him. His breathing was labored; his sides heaved with every breath. Medications no longer took away the pain. And so the time had come for losing a good pony on this day at Cherokee Hill, the name I gave to his burial ground.

On this heartbreaking day, I spoke to Cherokee softly through tears, while we said our farewell. He quietly waited while Wayne injected the liquid that would swiftly and humanely end his life. Spirit watched from above with my husband by his side, holding the horse's lead rope. Spirit's good-bye to Cherokee was silent to our ears.

Afterward, Spirit and I walked toward home. The rest of the herd milled around in an adjacent pasture and beckoned to us with soft and low whinnies. I removed Spirit's halter and lead rope, fully expecting him to rush and greet the other horses over the fence. He did not. Step by sad step, we trudged home together.

When the pain in my heart was too heavy, I would stop and lean on Spirit for emotional support. Mirroring to each other our pain and sorrow, the short trip across the field was an intuitive journey into our minds and hearts, as we felt and knew what each other was experiencing.

After Cherokee's passing, summer turned into winter. My thoughts returned to my studies. Here at Seasons Ranch, I spend the winters, my less active part of the year, studying different aspects of horse training and animal communication and behavior. It's a reflective time when my guest ranch and training center rest under a peaceful blanket of snow. The pasture transforms into cross-country ski trails.

One particularly quiet midwinter day, the sun shone stunningly over the hills. I decided to take a break from my studies and strap on my skis for a trip around the property. I had gone only a short distance and was near Cherokee Hill when I heard the urgent twittering of a chickadee. The bird buzzed over my head and landed on a branch almost within arm's reach.

The chickadee sat there, chattering, as I paused then flew ahead on the trail, still in the shadow of Cherokee Hill. There, the bird seemed to wait for me and again swooped over my head and landed on a branch so close that I could have touched him. The chickadee was definitely looking right at me and talking — chirping, cocking his head side to side. In this pasture, on a cold winter day it's unusual to even glimpse winter birds. It's typically quiet with only the occasional sound of very distant chittering. Other than this bird, the woods and hills were silent that day. This persistent chickadee and I were the only apparent life.

I continued to break trail with my skis and as if the bird was following me, I caught glimpses of him perching ahead of me in the trees. A quarter-mile farther on my walk near Cherokee Hill the chickadee came very close again. This time, he almost landed on my shoulder and then swept past to perch on a fencepost nearby. Again, the bird sang insistently before disappearing across the field. I was completely puzzled and almost could not believe such an amazing thing had happened.

My friend Barb came the following day to snowshoe, and we followed the same trail I had traveled the previous day. When we arrived at the place where the chickadee had appeared for the last time, I spotted something in the snow directly on our path ahead. As we approached, I recognized it as a bird's nest. Now, in addition to a lone chickadee flying, singing, and swooping close to me in the winter, here was a bird's nest. What was it doing in the middle of a field? No trees were around. Where had it come from?

Barb said, "Pick it up. Maybe it's good luck."

I put the deserted bird's nest in my backpack, and we continued on our walk. We were having a lovely time snowshoeing.

Barb does not come out often to visit, so we had much to catch up on. We made a campfire in the forest and thoroughly enjoyed ourselves. I didn't think to look more closely at the bird's nest until the next day when I emptied my backpack, pulled out the nest, and examined it. What I discovered brought me to an incredible realization and made me gasp. Artfully interwoven in the fine fibers of the nest were horsehairs. Not just any horsehairs, but Cherokee's mane or tail hair. Of all my horses, only he had a golden tinge to his hair, as distinct as the spots on his rump.

It dawned on me that my three visits from the chickadee had very special meaning. Finding a nest with Cherokee's hair woven into it in the middle of a field, on my path, was not a coincidence; it was a message from a very special horse. I am grateful that Cherokee found a way to let me know that he was fine and at peace. It lightened my heart.

Cherokee and I had trials and tests over the years. He wasn't an easy horse to ride when I got him. Many people told me to sell him immediately, but he reminded me to never to give up on a relationship and taught me patience and perseverance. He helped me to understand that to become a good rider sometimes requires taking a few falls, such as in life. Cherokee's health issues inspired me to help other horses. I have since studied, practiced, and now teach natural horse and hoof care.

I learned from Cherokee that it's not about the end result; it's about the journey. His last lesson was the most important of all. With his golden hair woven into the snowbound bird's nest, Cherokee taught me to believe in miracles. That day, I knew Cherokee wasn't really gone; he had only taken wing.

MEDITATION

The interplay of life and afterlife in Cherokee and Barbara's spiritual connection promises hope for all who have loved and lost a horse companion. In what golden nests have horse spirits hidden promises of reunion for you?

AFTERWORD

Horses have welcomed you to their hidden life through the stories in this book. They have revealed secrets that most people never know about them. The depth of their wisdom and compassion astounds. Powerful creatures with gentle souls and distinctive personalities, horses refuse classification. They fascinate and intrigue with their inscrutability. Every time people think they have horses all figured out, these complex creatures do something totally amazing.

Even though horses are unique individuals they have something in common: each horse serves in some way; every horse has a mission. Sometimes horses serve as symbols of courage, wisdom, hope, or forgiveness. Most often, horses create visions of independence and tranquility while humans ride atop their mighty backs and experience firsthand nature's bounty. In sports, the arts, and entertainment horses inspire with their athleticism, grace, and single-minded focus. Other horses answer their call to service by offering emotional healing — helping someone fulfill a lifelong dream, becoming the vehicle for a person's most important life lessons, reaching out to children with broken bodies and hearts and making them whole again, refusing to give up because a fellow creature still needs the light that an equine shines. The mission of wild horses and some domesticated ones is to guide us to remember history, cherish beauty for beauty's sake alone, and preserve the type of freedom we all aspire to attain.

Horses, like humans, are on journeys to greater self-awareness and expanded recognition of themselves as more than physical bodies. Their life experiences make them weaker or stronger, more shut down or open, kinder or meaner, slyer or truly wise. Although most of us can't get inside the minds of horses, anyone can read their body language, gaze into their eyes, and observe their actions. Horses tell us in no uncertain terms that if we treat them with the dignity they deserve and the love they crave, we will forge sublime spiritual partnerships that enrich both horse and human.

As prey animals and social beings who form families and express loyalty for their herds, horses have learned to protect and appreciate one another. The stories in this book demonstrate that horses are also adept at welcoming humans into their hearts. When given the opportunity and invitation to form loving and respectful relationships with people, horses freely give service in ways that go far beyond mere compliance.

We hope that even if you don't ride or associate with horses in your daily life, this book has opened you to dancing to the rhythm of their mighty hooves. Perhaps their greatest mission is to carry us into sacred places of the heart and soul that only a horse may enter.

ACKNOWLEDGMENTS

We give our appreciation to Georgia Hughes, New World Library's editorial director, who has worked with and encouraged us to bring to the world the messages in *Horses with a Mission*.

We are grateful to the wonderful visionary Marc Allen, the marketing director and associate publisher Munro Magruder, our enthusiastic and amazing publicity director Monique Muhlenkamp, managing editor Kristen Cashman, type designer Tona Pearce Myers, art director Mary Ann Casler, copy editor Pam Suwinsky, proofreader Gabriella West, editorial assistant Jonathan Wichmann, and all the staff at New World Library.

We sincerely appreciate the encouragement from Harold and Joan Klemp, who inspired us on our journey of giving service by writing books about the animal-human spiritual bond.

A special thanks to all the people who shared their stories about their many cherished experiences with horses.

We greatly appreciated the wisdom and generosity of judges for the 2008 Angel Horses with a Mission True Story Contest: Franklin Levinson, David Tucker, Crissy Tucker, Robin Cain, Shari Click, and Marcia Pruett Wilson. The contest became the rich resource for more than half of the stories in this book.

We extend our heartfelt gratitude to Stephanie Kip Rostan of Levine Greenberg Literary Agency, Inc., our energetic literary agent.

Our families instilled a love of animals in us from an early age. We especially appreciate Allen's mother, Bobbie Anderson, and Linda's mother, Gertrude Jackson. To our son and daughter, Mun Anderson and Susan Anderson: You're the best. Much love to Allen's sister, Gale Fipps, and brother, Richard Anderson, and their families.

Special thanks to Darby Davis, editor of *Awareness* magazine, for publishing our column, "Pet Corner," all these years, and to Kathy DeSantis and Sally Rosenthal for writing consistently beautiful book reviews. To Lessandra MacHamer: You have always been in our corner, and we love you for it.

And thanks to our current animal editors, Leaf, Speedy, Cuddles, and Sunshine. Without you, we wouldn't have been able to fulfill our purpose.

NOTES

Introduction

Epigraph: Julian Grenfell (1888–1915), "Into Battle," quoted in *The Columbia World of Quotations*, www.bartleby.com/66/68/26068.html (accessed February, 23, 2009).

1. "How We Shaped Horses, How Horses Shaped Us," American Museum of Natural History, www.amnh.org/exhibitions/horse/.
2. "Horses of the World: The Legacy of the Horse," International Museum of the Horse, Kentucky Horse Park, www.kyhorsepark.com/museum /history.php?chapter=112.
3. Sandra Chereb, "Equine Artist to Make International Debut in Italy," *USA Today*, October 15, 2008, www.usatoday.com/travel/destinations /2008-10-15-painting-horse_N.htm.
4. Renée Chambers, personal communication.
5. Jeanie and Tim Clifford, "B.I.T.S. History," Back in the Saddle Bit by Bit website, www.bitsbybit.org/history.html.
6. Meghan E. Moravcik, "Horses Used in Math Lesson," *Arizona Republic*, May 26, 2008, www.azcentral.com/news/articles/2008/05/26 /20080526edhorses0526.html.
7. "The Guide Horse Foundation Mission," Guide Horse Foundation — Miniature Horses for the Blind, www.guidehorse.com.
8. Marie Fasana, RN, MN, MA, "Holistic Inspiration," *Nurseweek*, July–August 2008, pp. 30–31.

9. Bill Leukhart, "World's Smallest Horse Gets a Dental Checkup," *Hartford Courant*, May 26, 2008, www.courant.com/news/local/hc-horse dentist.artmay26,0,4646514.story (accessed February, 23, 2009).

Chapter One: Offering Service

Epigraph: John Milton Hay (1838–1905), "The Stirrup Cup," in *Famous Poems from Bygone Days*, ed. Martin Gardner (Mineola, NY: Dover Publications, 1995), p. 87.

Chapter Two: Inspiring

Epigraph: Berton Braley, "Do It Now," quoted in the *Best Loved Poems of the American People*, Hazel Felleman, ed. (New York: Doubleday, 1936), p. 109.

Chapter Three: Teaching

Epigraph: Linda Kohanov, *The Tao of Equus: A Woman's Journey of Healing and Transformation through the Way of the Horse* (Novato, CA: New World Library, 2001), p. xvi. Published with permission of New World Library.

Chapter Four: Healing

Epigraph: Marty Becker, DVM, "Foreword" for *Angel Animals: Divine Messengers of Miracles* by Allen and Linda Anderson (Novato, CA: New World Library, 2007), p. xix. Published with permission of New World Library.

Chapter Five: Bringing Joy and Hope

Epigraph: 1 Corinthians 13:4–7, *Good News Bible, The Bible in Today's English Version*, under license from the American Bible Society (Nashville: Thomas Nelson, Inc., Publishers, 1976), pp. 1, 172.

Afterword

Epigraph: Jelaluddin Rumi (1207–1273), "The Dance of Your Hidden Life," *Rumi: Bridge to the Soul*, translations by Coleman Barks with A. J. Arberry and Nevit Ergin (New York: HarperOne, 2007), p. 92.

CONTRIBUTORS

Chapter One: Offering Service

VANESSA WRIGHT, "Under the Wings of Pegasus." Vanessa is an award-winning teacher, author, and equine photographer whose work celebrates the human-equine bond. Her internationally touring equestrian exhibit, The Literary Horse: When Legends Come to Life (www.TheLiteraryHorse.com) pairs photos of today's horses and horse-people with quotations from the world's great books. More than 100 of her photos and writings on horses have also been published through organizations ranging from Personal Ponies of Massachusetts to HCI Books. Vanessa holds an MEd from Harvard, a BA from the University of Chicago, and certification from the American Riding Instructors Association.

KAYE T. HARRIS, "Molly, the Three-Legged Pony Who Gave Hope to New Orleans." Kaye is founder and executive director of Kids and Ponies — Molly's Foundation. The nonprofit organization gratefully accepts donations at www.mollythepony.com. To see Molly's story and her in action visit www.myspace.com/mollythepony, www.lsu.edu/highlights/2006/10/molly.html, www.msnbc.msn.com/id/21134540/vp/25063046#25063046, and the *CBS Evening News* special "The Little Three-Legged Pony

That Could" at cbsnews.com/stories/2009/02/23/eveningnews /main4822620.shtml. Kaye can be reached at kidsandponies-molly @hotmail.com.

STEVE SCHWERTFEGER, "Birthing Frostbite, the Christmas Eve Foal." Steve lives in Crystal Lake, Illinois, with his family and is a humane investigator for the Hooved Animal Rescue and Protection Society, www.harpsonline.org. He feels thankfulness and love for both of his parents for encouraging him during his youth to care for animals. He is grateful that his dad moved the family out in the country and his mom always found time to help him with orphaned animals he seemed to constantly be caring for.

COOKY McCLUNG, "Old Pony Peanut Finds an Old Friend." Cooky has covered national and international equestrian competitions and capers for half a decade for *The Chronicle of the Horse, Horse Play, Practical Horse,* and *Horse Scene.* She currently writes for Phelps-SportsNetwork based in Wellington, Florida. She is the mother of seven children and grandmother of ten. Cooky is author of *Horsefolk Are Different* and *Horsefolk Are Still Different* (The Chronicle of the Horse, Inc., 1987 and 1995), *Plugly, the Horse That Could Do Everything* (Half Halt Press, 1993). She lives with her husband, Jim, in Chester County, Pennsylvania, where she continues to find endless fodder to pen equine escapades. Her story in this book was the grand prizewinner of the Angel Horses with a Mission True Story Contest. Cooky can be reached at goodlife@dejazzd.com.

Chapter Two: Inspiring

MILES J. DEAN, "Sankofa, the Horse Who Rewrote History." Miles is cofounder and executive director of the Black Heritage Riders, a New Jersey–based nonprofit organization dedicated to promoting initiatives that offer opportunities for enrichment in educational curriculums, particularly in the pre- and postcolonial periods in which horses serve as a symbol of the American frontier. Miles and his horse Sankofa completed A Modern African American Pioneer, a grueling cross-country educational odyssey with a virtual tour followed by millions of people. His goal is to increase self-esteem among African American children by drawing attention to the role African Americans played in the exploration, expansion, and settlement of the United States. www.milesdean.com.

KIMBERLY BLOSS, "Took Inspired Me to Rescue Morgans." Kimberly graduated with honors in English from State University of New York (SUNY) Cortland College. She is living her dream at Tantius Farm & Equine Sanctuary in upstate New York. www.tantiusfarm.com.

CHRISTIANNA E. CAPRA, "Finding My Passionate Purpose with Spring Thaw." Christianna is an Equine Assisted Growth and Learning Association (EAGALA)–certified equine specialist with more than thirty years of experience working with and riding horses. She is completing the requirements for advanced certification and currently building an equine-assisted psychotherapy (EAP) practice, called Spring Reins of Hope, in New Jersey, Pennsylvania, and New York. She lives and works in New York City and has more than fifteen years of sales, marketing, and public relations experience. She cohosts a monthly radio show, *Animal Matters: Reflections of Ourselves,* on www.healthandharmonyradio.com. Her horses, Spring Thaw and Dane, a nine-year-old Lipizzan-cross and competition horse, reside in New Jersey and are a big part of her life and happiness. cecapra@aol.com.

KIM MCELROY, "Avenger — Destiny Comes Full Circle." Kim is renowned for her equine art and writings. Her horse portraits, prints, books, gifts, and contact information are on her website, www.spiritofhorse.com. She can also be reached at Spirit of Horse Gallery, PO Box 1250, Kingston, WA 98346. To view Kim's inspiring flash movie/music horse ecards go to www.spiritofhorsecards.com.

Chapter Three: Teaching

KAREN SUSSMAN, "Diana: The Saga of a Wild Horse." Karen is president of International Society for the Protection of Mustangs and Burros (ISPMB), a nonprofit organization founded in 1960 and supported by volunteers and donations. She retired from her career as a nurse and after her children were grown she moved from Arizona to South Dakota to fulfill her dream of rescuing and preserving rare herds of wild horses that face elimination. Like Jane Goodall, Karen observes the wild horse herds' culture and family dynamics in their natural state and educates the world about her findings. www.ispmb.org.

ANNETTE FISHER, "Rocky, the Rescued Horse Who Is Changing a Community." Annette is executive director of Happy Trails Farm Animal Sanctuary, Inc., a 501(c)(3) nonprofit organization dedicated to spreading compassion and kindness for all animals, including farm animals and horses. www.happytrailsfarm.org, webinfo1@happytrailsfarm.org.

LAURA REDGRAVE, "Piper Led Me into the World of Horses." Laura was born in the San Francisco Bay Area of California. She hails from the distinguished Redgrave acting family. She was introduced into acting and modeling at age five and was a professional cheerleader for the Oakland Raiders for three years. Currently she resides in Los Angeles while pursuing real estate, photography, writing, and of course, acting and modeling. Two years after acquiring Piper, she rescued a rental-horse mustang named Austin. Laura's horse, Piper, was foaled in Oklahoma as Ozark's Dunny Girl. Piper is a registered American Quarter Horse. Her great-grand-sires are Three Bars and Blondy's Dude. Piper trained as a polo pony in Santa Barbara, California, prior to Laura finding her.

KAREN KUKLA SPIES, "Finding Balance with Blondie." Karen lives in the San Francisco Bay Area with her husband of fifteen years, Larry; their daughter, Katie; and their Cavalier King Charles spaniel, Murphy. Karen is a mediator and avid horseback rider.

Chapter Four: Healing

JODI BUCHAN, "Butch, the Horse Who Believed in My Daughter." Jodi has been a merchandiser, advocate, and writer. She is currently working on the story of a mother's metamorphosis, *Normal: A Mythical Memoir*.

TANYA K. WELSCH, MSW, LGSW, "Viola, Wise Mother Mare." As a licensed social worker and cofounder of the nonprofit Minnesota Linking Individuals, Nature & Critters, Inc. (MN LINC), Tanya incorporates the human-animal-nature bond in her work with youth, families, and human services agencies. Tanya is a coauthor of four manuals that provide animal- and nature-based activities. She teaches a yearlong professional development course in animal-assisted therapy and education, is a Pet Partners team evaluator with the Delta Society, a board member of Equine Facilitated Mental Health Association, and TTeam practitioner-in-training through Tellington TTouch. View a video of Viola and Tanya in action at www.startribune.com/video/11534361.html?elr=KArks :DCiUBDia_nDaycUiacyKUU. For more information on MN LINC, go to www.mnlinc.org.

SALLY HEINS, "Riley's Greatest Gift." Sally is the lead vet tech for the large animal departments at Best Friends Animal Society in Kanab, Utah (www.bestfriends.org). She is devoted to her work in sanctuary medicine and animal rescue. This work can be exhausting, but it provides her with the rewarding sense of satisfaction that comes from pursuing a meaningful cause. Sally shares her home with a three-pound, small but tough, rescued Maltese mix, Lilly Jane, and the diverse personalities and entertaining antics of her cats. Sally can be reached at sally.heins@gmail.com. To read more about Sally's tribute to Riley and her mission, go to www.bestfriends.org/guardianangel.

MARY HILL, "Saved by My Li'l Man." Mary "Maizie" Hill is a native of Pennsylvania but a longtime Maryland resident. She has been married to her actor husband, Reid Hill, for more than twenty-five years. Mary has been a horse owner since 1968 and enjoys practicing the Parelli Natural Horsemanship program.

MEAGHAN MARTIN, "Charlie, the White Marble Statue Healer." Meaghan is a seventeen-year-old musician and equestrian. She's a friend to people and horses alike and is always chasing her dreams with everything in her heart. Meaghan has started a campaign with her horse, Charlie, using the scores they earn at dressage competitions to support breast cancer research at the Maine Medical Center Research Institute. http://ribbonsforribbons.tripod.com.

Chapter Five: Bringing Joy and Hope

SHEILA ANDERSON, "Chevy's Compassion." Sheila still belongs to Chevy, and they have retired in Colorado, where he is happy and healthy. He enjoys trail rides and his BFF (best friend forever) Sundance. Sheila is currently an equine artist. www.paloose-arts.com.

PAULINE PETERSON, "Traveling to the Place on Peen's Breath." Pauline is a registered nurse and a Minnesota author and columnist for *Horse'n Around* magazine. She is author of *Horses for Pauline* (Hoofbeat Press, Box 484, Castle Rock, MN 55010), a compilation of her columns published over a five-year period. Pauline began riding dude ranch horses as a teenage city slicker. www.pauline peterson.com.

SAM YOUNGHANS, "Asleep with Saki." Sam grew up with dogs and horses. He always thought everyone talked to the animals, because it was so natural for him to do so. The animals Sam has known taught him love, faithfulness, patience, and humility. The spirits of those friends remain with him to this day. Sam loves to write and is never without the inspiration he gets from his memories. Bogwig.com features his latest project, an illustrated version of his book *Cancel Christmas* (Pinnacle-Syatt Publications, 1996) and a stage play by the same name.

BARBARA FENWICK, "Cherokee Took Wing." Barbara teaches natural horse and hoof care. Her holistic horsemanship program is Freedom with Horses. She believes that horses are wonderful teachers. We just need to listen, watch, and believe. www.barb fenwick.com.

ADDITIONAL PHOTOGRAPHERS

Except for the following, the photographs accompanying each story in this book were taken by the contributing authors.

ABOUT ALLEN AND LINDA ANDERSON

Allen and Linda Anderson are speakers and authors of a series of books about the spiritual relationships between people and animals. Their mission is to help people discover and benefit from the miraculous powers of animals. In 1996, they cofounded the Angel Animals Network.

In 2004, Allen and Linda Anderson were recipients of a Certificate of Commendation in recognition of their contributions as authors in the state of Minnesota.

In 2007, their book *Rescued: Saving Animals from Disaster* won the American Society of Journalists and Authors Outstanding Book award.

Allen Anderson is a writer and photographer. He was profiled in Jackie Waldman's book *The Courage to Give*. Linda Anderson is an award-winning playwright as well as a screenwriter and fiction writer. She is the author of *Thirty-Five Golden Keys to Who You Are & Why You're Here*. Allen and Linda teach writing at the Loft Literary Center in Minneapolis, where Linda was awarded the Anderson Residency for Outstanding Loft Teachers.

The Andersons share their home with a dog, two cats, and a cockatiel. They donate a portion of revenue from their projects to animal shelters and animal welfare organizations.

You are welcome to visit Allen and Linda's website at www.angelanimals.net and their homepages and groups on Facebook (search "Linda-Allen Anderson"), Beliefnet (Angel Pets Fan Club), and other social networking sites. They invite you to send them stories and letters about your experiences with animals. At the website or by email, you may also request a subscription to their free email newsletter, *Angel Animals Story of the Week*, which features inspiring stories about animals around the world.

Contact Allen and Linda Anderson at:
Angel Animals Network
PO Box 26354
Minneapolis, MN 55426
www.angelanimals.net
www.horseswithamission.com
angelanimals@angelanimals.net

HELPING TO PRESERVE OUR ENVIRONMENT

46,104
trees were saved

New World Library uses 100% postconsumer-waste
recycled paper for our books whenever possible, even if it costs more.
During 2008 this choice saved the following precious resources:

www.newworldlibrary.com

ENERGY	WASTEWATER	GREENHOUSE GASES	SOLID WASTE
32 MILLION BTU	17 MILLION GAL.	4 MILLION LB.	2 MILLION LB.

Environmental impact estimates were made using the Environmental Defense Fund Paper Calculator @ www.papercalculator.org.